AN INTRODUCTION TO CHRISTIAN THEOLOGY

An Introduction to CHRISTIAN Theology

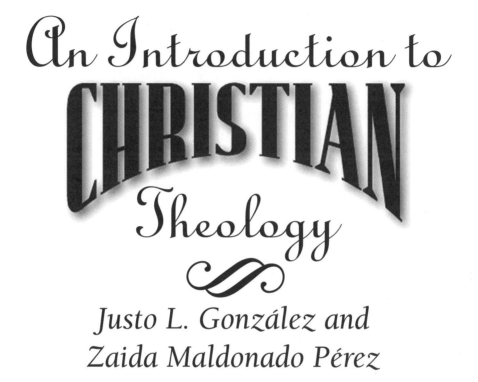

Justo L. González and
Zaida Maldonado Pérez

Abingdon Press
Nashville

AN INTRODUCTION TO CHRISTIAN THEOLOGY

Copyright © 2002 by Abingdon Press

This book is printed on acid-free paper.

Library of Congress Cataloging-in-Publication Data

González, Justo L.
  An introduction to Christian theology / Justo L. González and Zaida Maldonado Pérez.
    p. cm.
Includes bibliographical references.
  ISBN 0-687-09573-5 (pbk. : alk. paper)
  1. Theology, Doctrinal. I. Maldonado Pérez, Zaida, 1957- II. Title.
BT65 .G66 2002
230—dc21

                                                                                2002004628

02 03 04 05 06 07 08 09 10 11—10 9 8 7 6 5 4 3 2 1

MANUFACTURED IN THE UNITED STATES OF AMERICA

CONTENTS

PREFACE

In a way, this book is the result of a request to its authors from the Association for Hispanic Theological Education (AETH), for a simple book that could be used as introductory reading for those who are barely taking their first steps in the field of theology. But it is also the result of the authors' experience, when we were students, of having to plunge into theological studies without the help of a concise introduction to the field. As we reflected on that request, we set for ourselves several requirements or goals:

First of all, the book should be easily read and understood. One of the main difficulties facing beginning students of theology is the difficult language and style of much of the material they are invited to read.

Second, the book should stimulate reflection rather than offering answers that students can memorize. Indeed, one of the main shortcomings of many introductory books on theology is that they offer ready-made answers, without alerting the reader to the existence of other alternatives or positions.

Third, the book should serve as an introduction, not to the theology of a particular denomination or school, but to the fuller spectrum of Christian theology as it has developed through the centuries. Certainly, since we have written it, the book will show our preferences and inclinations; but we have made an effort to be fair to other positions and perspectives. On one point the reader will note, however, that we have allowed our particular bias to show. We are both historians, and are convinced that the best approach to theology is through its history—that theology always builds on the shoulders of those who have gone before. Therefore, rather than focusing our attention on issues of contemporary theology, we have sought to provide readers with some of the necessary background to place those issues in their proper historical context.

Fourth, as an *introduction*, the book should show the student that there is much more to be studied, and that the surface has barely been skimmed. As a sign in this direction, the text is printed in two different sizes of type. We have endeavored to produce a book that can be read at two different levels. Those who merely wish to follow the general argument will find that it is possible to read only the large type as a continuous text. Those who desire more detail or further clarification will find it in the smaller type. Also, as a further aid to the reader, we have added at the end a brief list of Authors Cited, which will help place references to such authors in their wider historical and theological context.

Finally, a word of gratitude. Since theology is always built on the shoulders of predecessors, those to whom we are indebted are indeed a great cloud of witnesses. However, at a more immediate level, we wish to express our gratitude to our spouses, Catherine and Luis, who are both also theologically trained, and who have helped us in uncountable ways. To them, sure signs of the love with which God surrounds us, and to the God of all love, we offer a heartfelt *¡gracias!*

I. WHAT IS THEOLOGY?

The most common approach to this question is to examine the roots of the word *theology*. Thus, we are told that *theology* comes from two Greek roots: *theos*, which means "God," and *logos*, which means "study, reason, or treatise." In conclusion, theology is the discipline that studies God. That is what many introductory books say, and to a certain point it is true.

However, the truth is that when we declare that theology is "the discipline that studies God," we have not said much. Each intellectual discipline defines its own method on the basis of the object it studies. Physics is based on the observation of the manner in which physical bodies behave, and astronomy on the observation of the movement of the heavenly bodies. Mathematics is an abstract discipline, which does not really base its findings on any observation, but only on abstract arithmetic quantities, geometric forms, and so forth. History cannot look directly at the events that it discusses, and therefore studies documents, archaeological remains, and other pointers to those events. In short, each discipline must develop its own method, and that method must somehow relate to the theme or subject of its study.

Looking now at theology, we soon realize that it is not enough to say that theology is "the discipline that studies God." It is also necessary to take into account who this God is whom theology studies, and how this God is known. This will be discussed in the next chapter, but for the present one can say at least that God is known through divine revelation—a statement that in itself is of the utmost importance for theology.

Furthermore, the methods each discipline follows are closely related to its purpose. Some disciplines have both a purely intellectual or cognitive purpose and a practical one. Meteorology, for example, studies the atmospheric phenomena in order not only to understand them better, but also in order to foretell them and thus help us be better prepared for storms, droughts, and so on. History, which at first sight might appear to be the unbiased study of past events, in truth also seeks to understand and interpret the present, and to point toward the future. Even astronomy, which studies distant bodies, also seeks to help us understand the tides, radiation, and solar storms and their impact on radio transmission. Likewise, when we ask, What is theology? we are also asking about its use, about its purpose.

For all these reasons, in the rest of this chapter we will begin by asking what is the purpose of theology, in order then to move to other subjects that will help us understand what theology is and how it is done.

1. THE FUNCTION OF THEOLOGY

Throughout history, those who have devoted themselves to theology have understood their task in various ways.

(a) Theology as an explanation of reality

It was thus that the word *theology* was first employed, even centuries before the birth of Jesus. The ancient Greeks gave the title "theologians" to the poets and other authors who explained the origins of things through myths about the gods. In the Christian church, theology also sometimes has been understood as an explanation of reality, and this has often brought dire consequences. For example, when Galileo first suggested that the sun did not revolve around the earth, as was believed in his time, ecclesiastical authorities condemned him, because his explanation of reality did not coincide with that of the "theologians." Although it is true that the Christian faith, and therefore also theology, offers us an understanding of reality, this is not so much an explanation of how things work, or how they originated, as it is a view of their place in God's purposes. As we shall see later on, not to distinguish between these two approaches to reality is to create confusion between theology and the physical sciences. When that happens, we run the risk of holding the Christian faith hostage to the vicissitudes and the evolving views and discoveries of those sciences.

The case of Galileo serves as a warning about the dangers in this view of theology. If theology is the explanation of the functioning of reality, every other intellectual discipline has to submit to it. That is why medieval theologians often claimed that their discipline was the "queen of the sciences." Some theologians held that the earth was the physical center of the universe because Joshua 10:13 says that both the sun and the moon stood still. Therefore, no astronomer had the right to claim the contrary, and this led to the condemnation of Galileo. Today we agree that Galileo was right. Therefore, one must beware of any theology or biblical interpretation that seeks to explain how things are, how they work, and so forth. Theology certainly does affirm that all that exists has been created by God, and that everything has a place in God's plan. But how these things function is a matter of concern for other disciplines, and not for theology.

Perhaps the point at which this understanding of theology and its danger are most clearly seen today is the manner in which some read the narratives in Genesis as scientific explanations of the origin of things and animals. Such a reading of Genesis, which sees in it the literal history of the origin of things, clashes not only with today's scientific theories—which after all are no more than theories—but with Genesis itself. In Genesis 1, we are told that God first created the animals and finally the human beings, both male and female, while in Genesis 2 the order is quite different: God creates first the man, then the animals, and finally the woman. Were we to read the narratives of Genesis as scientific descriptions, we would face the need to declare that Genesis contradicts itself.

This is not to say that theology has nothing to do with the sciences. On the contrary, theology must take into account all human knowledge, and it must also be ready to speak of how various scientific procedures and options must be judged in the light of the gospel. Thus, biology itself cannot determine whether the cloning of humans ought to be done or not, but in this regard requires the guidance of ethics—including theological ethics.

(b) Theology as the systematization of Christian doctrine

From a very early date in the history of Christianity, the need was apparent to systematize the teachings of the Christian faith, or at least its main tenets. Already by the middle of the second century there was a "rule of faith," which was a short summary of those essential tenets, emphasizing those which were denied by some individual or group.

Toward the end of that century and early in the third, the great systematizer of Christian doctrine was Origen, whose work *On First Principles* deals with all the central themes of Christianity, from the doctrine of God and creation to eschatology. Ever since, hundreds of "systematic theologies" have been written, whose purpose is precisely to present Christian doctrine as an ordered and coherent whole.

This function of theology is important, although it too has its dangers. As a systematization of Christian doctrine, it can serve as a point of reference from which to weigh and judge any doctrine or idea that may be suggested. It was thus that the ancient church used the "rule of faith." If somebody suggested that a certain thing had been created not by God but by the Enemy, it was easy to respond rather quickly that the rule of faith affirms that God is "maker of heaven and earth" or "creator of all things, visible and invisible." The same was true if someone denied eternal life, or the incarnation of God in Jesus Christ.

This function of theology is also valid for us today. If, in the course of a Bible study in a church, someone suggests an interpretation of a text that contradicts the message of the rest of the Bible, and we have studied theology, that theological knowledge will help us recognize and correct the error in what is being proposed, and help us seek a possible different interpretation of the text.

This view and use of theology also involves its perils. The most serious is the possibility that we may be so intent in systematizing and classifying everything that we give the resultant theological system an authority that is far beyond its due.

This was the great danger of much systematic theology in the nineteenth century, and it was against this excessive systematization that Danish Lutheran theologian Søren Kierkegaard insisted that the human being, simply because it exists, because it is placed within time and space, can never systematize all reality. He says, "Does this mean that there is no such system? Certainly not. All of reality is a system for God; but never for us." (Author's translation)

Another example of such thorough and excessive systematization may be seen in the matter in which Calvinist theologian Jerome Zanchi, late in the sixteenth century, tried to prove the doctrine of predestination. He claims that since God is both omnipotent and omniscient—that is, can do all things and knows all things—God knows and determines what is to take place, which leaves no room for human freedom. What Zanchi has done with such an argument is to make us believe that God has to fit within our own narrow understanding of omniscience and omnipotence. But the truth is that, if God is truly omnipotent, God does not have to fit the arguments of Zanchi or any other theologian. If God is truly omniscient, God will know how to allow for human freedom, even though Zanchi's "system" ultimately leaves no room for it.

Another danger in such an excessive system of theology is that the message and work of God may appear to be reduced to three or four points in such a system. This is what happens, for example, when people reduce the message of the Bible to a "plan of salvation" consisting of three, four, or a dozen points, and give the impression that knowing such points is sufficient, so the rest of the Bible is no longer really necessary.

(c) Theology as the defense of the faith, and as a bridge for nonbelievers

From a very early date the church felt the need to defend the faith against those who criticized it, as well as to prepare the way for nonbelievers to approach the gospel in a manner that made sense to them. Thus, when the Christian church began teaching in the midst of the Roman Empire and its Greco-Roman culture, there were some who mocked Christians because they had no visible god. To respond to such criticism, some Christian intellectual leaders began seeking bridges or points of contact between their faith and the surrounding culture. This they found in what some of the most distinguished philosophers of antiquity—especially Plato— had said about the Supreme Being. According to these philosophers, above all visible beings there must be a first Being, infinite and immutable, from which all other beings derive their existence. Joining that ancient philosophical assertion with Christian doctrine, those early Christian theologians—people such as Justin

Martyr, Clement of Alexandria, and Origen—claimed that the same Being whom the Christians called "God" or "Father" was the one whom the ancient philosophers called the "Supreme Being," "Highest Beauty," "Supreme Goodness," or "Prime Mover." Thus they showed its critics that Christian belief was not as senseless as was claimed, and that Christians, far from being "atheists," worshiped a Being far beyond all the pretended pagan gods.

This is usually called the "apologetic function" of theology. In this context, "apology" means "defense." Therefore, the first Christian writers who wrote this sort of theological writing are called "apologists." For the same reason, theology that seeks to serve this function is usually called "apologetic theology" or simply "apologetics."

There is no doubt that this function of theology is important and valuable. Had it not been for those early apologists of the second century, and for those who continued their work thereafter, Christianity would not have been able to dialogue with the surrounding culture. Already in the book of Acts, we see first Peter, then Stephen, and finally Paul, who are all Jews, defending the Christian faith before other Jews who do not accept it. Today, since there are so many arguments and prejudices against Christian faith, it is necessary to refute them, if not necessarily in order to prove that Christianity is true, at least in order to remove the false obstacles that are placed in the path to faith. In its apologetic function, theology may help us refute the argument of those atheists who claim that it is unreasonable to believe in God.

Apologetic theology also has its dangers. We shall see some of those when we deal with the "proofs" for the existence of God in the next chapter. At any rate, part of the danger is that every apologetic argument is like a bridge that may carry traffic in both directions: it can serve not only to convince nonbelievers of the acceptability of Christianity, but also to convince believers that their faith corresponds to much in the general culture, and to do this in ways that may affect the content of their belief.

A clear example of this appears already in the arguments of the apologists of the second century, to whom we have already referred, and the manner in which their thought has influenced the Christian doctrine of God. When those apologists faced Greco-Roman culture, they felt the need to defend their belief in a single and invisible God over against a culture that believed in many gods and saw them in the statues placed in the temples and elsewhere. In order to respond to such a situation, the apologists had recourse to the teachings of Plato regarding the Supreme Being, and then they claimed that that Being was the God of Christianity. Obviously, the great asset in that argument was in that it claimed for the proclamation of the Christian faith the support of one of the most respected and admired thinkers of antiquity. The great liability was the possibility that Christians might come to the conclusion—which they did—that the manner in which Plato spoke of the Supreme Being was better or more precise than the manner in which the Bible speaks of God. In consequence, much of Christian theology began to think of God as an impersonal, impassible being, removed from human reality, and therefore very different from the God of Israel and of Jesus Christ, who intervenes and partakes in human history, who suffers with the suffering, and responds to prayers.

(d) Theology as a critique of the life and proclamation of the church

Another way of understanding the function of theology is to see it as a critique of the life and proclamation of the church in the light of the gospel. The church is commanded to proclaim the gospel and to live it. It is a task that we undertake even while acknowledging our incompetence and insufficiency for it. As sinful human beings, our words are always very far from being the Word of God. As a human institution, the church also carries the mark of human sin and fallibility. It is only by God's grace—God's self-giving love—that our words may convey a word from God. It is only by God's grace that our actions can point toward God's purpose. It is only by God's grace that the proclamation of the church can become proclamation of the Word of God, and the organizations and acts of the church may point to God's reign.

In spite of our fallibility and of our constant dependence on the grace of God, we still must do all we can in order to make our words and actions reflect the Word and purposes of God. That is the function of theology as critique of the proclamation and the life of the church. As critique of the proclamation of the church, theology examines what the church says, and seeks to judge and correct it in the light of the gospel—not in order to criticize it in the negative sense of the word, but in order to bring it to greater faithfulness to the gospel. Thus, theology may be one of the criteria by which we evaluate our sermons, our lessons, and our writings in order to make certain that—in the measure to which such is possible—our words are faithful to the gospel.

As critique of the life of the church, theology examines what the church does and how it organizes its own life, and judges it in the light of the gospel, not to criticize it, but in order to call the church to greater faithfulness to the faith it claims. In preparing the budget of a church, or in determining its structures or systems of government, we must ask: *How does this reflect the gospel of Jesus Christ?* That is precisely the function of theology as critique of the life of the church.

The twentieth-century theologian who became best known for proposing such an understanding of theology was Karl Barth. Barth lived in a time in which theology had become a series of intellectual and doctrinal systems that may have had great apologetic value, and which in some quarters made Christianity appear quite acceptable, but which had little to say about the life and mission of the church. This became particularly clear at the time of the rise of Nazism, when many German Christians followed the general mood of the nation, and even preached it from the pulpit, and when most of the German church was unable to resist it. At that point, Barth insisted on the function of theology as critique of the life and proclamation of the church. A church that proclaimed and supported Nazi doctrines needed to submit to the critique of theology, showing it that it was being unfaithful to the gospel that it was supposed to be proclaiming.

Today, such a function of theology is still necessary. For instance, when the church and Christians seem to ignore the poor, or when they begin to say that all that is important is "success" in life, or that Christian faith leads to "prosperity," or whenever they seem to bow before the latest cultural fad, theology must call them to a new obedience to the gospel.

The main danger in such an understanding of theology is the possibility that it may become ecclesiocentric. If it is a function of theology to critique the proclamation and life of the church, does it not have anything to say to those who are not part of the church? In the worst cases, such theology becomes a conversation among theologians, or among Christians, as if the rest of the world did not exist or matter. Clearly, what happens in such cases is that we have forgotten that what theology is to critique is the *proclamation* of the church, that is, its encounter with the rest of the world. If theology does not call the church to such an encounter, it would appear that theology itself is in need of the critique that is supposed to be its own function.

(e) Theology as contemplation

Another way of understanding theology, which was very common in ancient times, but which modernity seems to have forgotten, is theology as contemplation. When someone was called a "theologian" what was often meant was what today we call a "mystic." That is why from a very early date it became customary to call the author of the book of Revelation "John the Theologian." That is also why in the ancient church the title of "theologian" was usually reserved for those believers and writers whose spirit of contemplation was exceptional.

The value of this emphasis on "contemplation" as an essential part of theology is that it counteracts the modern tendency to think that theology is just one more intellectual discipline, and that in order to pursue it, it suffices to study it. In speaking of theology as "contemplation," one underlines the devotional character of theology—of a discipline that must be pursued not only sitting behind a desk, but also kneeling before an altar. That is why in the fourth century, Gregory of Nazianzus, one of the first authors to ask the question of the nature of theology, says that one of the first steps of a theologian must be "to polish one's own theological being until it shines like a statue." (Speeches, 27.7)

There is also the danger, especially in our highly individualistic time and society, of understanding theology in such a way that we become entrapped in private visions. When this happens, anyone who claims to have had a vision also has the right to claim theological authority. Although there is no doubt that throughout the history of the church visions have had a function, it is also true that throughout that history the church has had to find ways to protect itself and its believers from the consequences of supposed private revelations that contradict the gospel. In order to preserve the view of theology as contemplation from such dangers, it is important to remember the relationship between theology and the community of faith, to which we shall return.

Perhaps the most viable view of theology as contemplation is expressed in the phrase "faith seeking understanding," connected with the work of Anselm of Canterbury in the twelfth century. According to this view, what theology seeks to do is to gain a deeper understanding and intellectual appreciation for what one already believes. Thus, Anselm sets out to prove the existence of God, not because he needs such proof in order to believe, but because his love for God is such that he must employ his mind in order to understand as much as possible. In this case theology becomes a sort of contemplation, although not the somewhat amorphous contemplation of some mystics, but rather the intellectually rigorous contemplation of a devoted scholar.

In summary, theology and its function can be understood in various ways. Most of these are not mutually exclusive, but rather complement one another. Probably, given the present situation in the church, we should emphasize theology as critique of the life and proclamation of the church, although at the same time allowing for theology as systematization of doctrine, as a bridge toward nonbelievers, and as contemplation.

2. THEOLOGY AND PHILOSOPHY

For a number of reasons, throughout the history of the church there has been a close relationship between theology and philosophy. So much so, that in several Christian traditions it is customary to require that people study philosophy as preparation for the study of theology. That traditional relationship between the two disciplines is because of a number of reasons: (1) Both seem to study the same subject. Theology, as well as some philosophical schools, deals with the meaning of life, ethical values, ultimate reality, and so on. (2) Both seem to be relatively abstract disciplines. (3) Philosophy seems to be an ideal introduction to theology. There are also reasons to suspect that philosophy may cause theology to err, and that therefore it is best to separate the two disciplines.

The manner in which we view the relationship between philosophy and theology is in itself a theological question, since it depends on the position we take on the nature and function of theology. Therefore, throughout the history of the church there have been different positions regarding philosophy and its place in relation to theology, running the gamut from those who see the two as enemies to those who see them as allies.

(a) Philosophy and theology in opposition

According to this view, all that philosophy has to contribute to theology is error. Theology must be completely independent from philosophy, because when it is not, it allows itself to be guided by demonic powers, or at least by a human reason that is twisted as the result of sin.

There were those in the ancient church who felt that many or perhaps most of the doctrinal errors circulating among Christians were because of philosophy. The best known of those who held this position was Tertullian, who lived in North Africa toward the end of the second century and early in the third. Tertullian was concerned over the various doctrines circulating in his time, particularly those of the Gnostics and of Marcion, which seemed to contradict essential aspects of the gospel. Some held that only spiritual reality was good, and that therefore God was not the creator of the physical world. Some denied the reality of the physical body of Jesus. Some claimed that God's love is such that God never judges or punishes. Tertullian was convinced that the origin of all such ideas was in philosophy. Therefore, speaking of Athens and its Academy as symbols of philosophy, he declared, "What indeed has Athens to do with Jerusalem? What concord is there between the Academy and the Church?" (Tertullian, *Prescription Against Heretics*)

At other times, other theologians have held similar positions. In the twentieth century, Karl Barth, who has already been mentioned, rejected the use of philosophy in theology. This was partly because of the manner in which several thinkers in the generations immediately preceding Barth produced systems in which theology and philosophy were confused and even indistinguishable. It was also because of Barth's understanding of theology and its purpose, which required the autonomy of theology, and therefore its independence from philosophy or any other discipline.

(b) Philosophy and theology coincide

At all times there have been theologians who have insisted that, since truth is one, philosophy and theology are ultimately dealing with the same reality, and what they say is either identical or very similar. Characteristically, such theologians tend to take the philosophy that is in vogue in their time and show how it coincides with Christian faith.

Such was the position of Origen in the third century vis-à-vis Platonism, that of John Scotus Erigena in the ninth vis-à-vis Neoplatonism, that of many theologians vis-à-vis Hegel in the nineteenth, and in the twentieth century that of Rudolf Bultmann vis-à-vis existentialism.

(c) Philosophy and theology as complementary

The third position that has been common among Christian theologians places itself between the two extremes that have just been mentioned. This third option sees philosophy and theology as complementary, with philosophy serving as an introduction to theology.

As examples of two different ways in which such a relationship between theology and philosophy is understood and justified, Justin Martyr and Thomas Aquinas are paramount. Justin Martyr was the most important apologist of the second century. In his *Apology*, he undertook the task of showing how and why Christianity could claim for itself the best in ancient philosophy. He did this on the basis of the doctrine of the *Logos* or "Word." Greek philosophers had explained that if the human mind can understand the universe, the reason for this is that there is a common principle of rationality in both the mind and the universe, the *Logos*. All that humans know, they know by virtue of this *Logos*, which inspires that knowledge in them. Since the Fourth Gospel says that in Jesus the *Logos* or the Word of God was made flesh (John 1:14), Justin claims that all any human being at any time has known, has come to that person through the inspiration of the same Word that was incarnate in Jesus. Therefore, Christians can take for themselves all that the ancient philosophers knew, for this is a revelation of the same *Logos* or Word. However, since Christians have seen the Word made flesh, their knowledge is higher and more precise than that of the philosophers.

Such use of the doctrine of the *Logos* or Word has been frequent in Christian theology in various times. In the fourth and fifth centuries, Augustine used it as the foundation for his theory of human knowledge. In the thirteenth, Bonaventura wrote a treatise under the title of *Christ, the Sole Teacher of All* in which he claims that "the light of the created mind [that is, the human mind] does not suffice to understand anything without the light of the eternal word."

Thomas Aquinas lived in the thirteenth century, when Aristotelian philosophy was beginning to make headway in western Europe. He insisted that truth is only one, and that therefore any knowledge that philosophy acquires cannot contradict what is known by theology. One could outline his position saying that philosophy, by means of reason, ascends toward truth, whereas in theology truth descends by means of revelation. The consequence is that theological truth is more certain than philosophical conclusion, and therefore when there seems to be a contradiction between the two, one must conclude that philosophical reason has erred. But it also means that philosophy, since it proceeds on the basis of reason, produces an understanding of truth that is deeper than that which is accepted by the authority of revelation. There are certain truths, such as the doctrine of the Trinity, that can only be known by revelation, and that therefore belong only in the field of theology. There are other truths that are not necessary for salvation, and which therefore are neither revealed nor a proper subject for theology. But there are still others, such as the existence of God, which may be known by reason, but are also necessary for salvation. Such truths God has revealed, so that salvation will not depend on reason and its conclusions, or on a person's intellectual ability.

To a significant extent, the manner in which one conceives the function of theology determines the manner in which one conceives its relation with philosophy. If theology is above all an explanation of reality, it is easy to confuse it with philosophy, which is one of those explanations. This was what took place when the philosophy of Hegel seemed to have developed a system that explained all of reality, and the theologians who followed that philosophy were hardly able to distinguish between that system and their own Christian theology. If theology is above all apology, philosophy becomes particularly important, for it is the bridge that serves to convince nonbelievers of the truth of the Christian faith. If theology is above all a critique of the life and the proclamation of the church, philosophy is no more than one of the many elements in the world in which the church lives and where its proclamation takes place.

3. THEOLOGY AND THE PHYSICAL AND NATURAL SCIENCES

Beginning in the fifteenth century, an entire series of discoveries took place in the Western world, and these produced radical changes in the way in which the universe was conceived. No longer did the sun rotate around the earth. The world was no longer composed of three parts, which until then had been seen as a vestige of the Trinity: Europe, Asia, and Africa. Now disease began to be understood differently, with the discovery of microbes, hormones, and genes. The natural sciences—such as zoology, biology, physics, and astronomy—opened horizons that revolutionized the universe, from the particles forming the atom to the movement of the celestial bodies.

This frequently resulted in conflicts with theology, especially with that sort of theology that saw itself as an explanation of reality. If, for instance, theology "knows" that the sun and all the heavenly bodies rotate around the earth, it must necessarily oppose the new astronomic views. If it "knows" that disease is due primarily to demons, it will not be able to accept modern medicine. If it "knows" that God made the world in exactly six days, it will not be able to accept or to understand the discoveries of paleontology.

Thus, the manner in which we see the relationship between theology and the natural sciences will depend on our view of the function of theology. If it is a description of reality, the conflict with the natural sciences will be unavoidable. If it is systematization of Christian doctrine, defense of the faith, or critique of the proclamation of the church, the conflict will be different, or will not exist at all.

It is important to remember that theology is indeed interested in the physical realities that the natural sciences study. Such doctrines as creation, incarnation, and others tell us that God is concerned and involved with the physical universe and the human body. Therefore, theology must also be interested in that universe, and must take into account what the physical and natural sciences tell us about it.

A phrase that was often employed in order to explain the relationship between theology and the other intellectual disciplines is that *theology is the queen of sciences*. This was justified on the basis that, since theology deals with God, who reigns over the universe, theology must reign over all the sciences, which deal with mere creatures. Naturally, such an understanding of theology has been part of the conflicts just described. However, if we remember that God reigns above creatures, not as a tyrant, but as a God of love, and that God's rule is manifested above all in the cross, we must conclude that, if indeed theology reigns in any sense, this would only be true inasmuch as it becomes a servant of all other disciplines.

4. THEOLOGY AND THE HUMAN AND SOCIAL SCIENCES

During the nineteenth century, and especially in the twentieth, a number of relatively new disciplines developed, many of which had not previously attained the category of sciences. Anthropology, psychology, sociology, and economy, for instance, although finding their roots in ancient times, have become scientific disciplines in modern times. This in its turn poses the question of the relationship between theology and these disciplines. For a time it was thought that these new sciences had nothing to do with theology, because after all theology—as well as philosophy—deals with eternal truths, and the truths of these new sciences are, in the best of cases, temporary and circumstantial. However, these disciplines and their conclusions do relate to theology, for at least two reasons.

(a) Theology is concerned with human reality

Were theology only interested in the divine nature, it could possibly ignore the social sciences. However, if theology has to do with the life and proclamation of the church, and if the church must carry forth its proclamation in a human context, these human sciences become extremely important. In order to understand the context in which the church lives and proclaims, as well as the very nature of the church itself, the social and human sciences are indispensable. Furthermore, in its task of critiquing the proclamation and the life of the church in the light of the gospel, theology has repeatedly pointed out that the church cannot forget the human, economic, and social dimensions of the biblical witness. In the Bible, the people of God are repeatedly told that they must take care of the defenseless, such as widows, orphans, the alien, and the poor (Exod. 22:21-23; 23:9; Lev. 19:9-10; 23:22; Deut. 14:29; 24:17-22; 27:19; Isa. 1:17; Jer. 7:6; 22:3; Ezek. 22:7, 29; Zech. 7:10; Mal. 3:5; Mark 12:40; Luke 20:47; James 1:17). What is more, this is not only a matter of ethics, for it reflects the very nature of God, who is particularly interested in the defenseless (Deut. 11:17-19; Pss. 10:14, 18; 68:5-6). All this implies that if theology is to call the church to obedience, it must seek to understand as much as possible of the human reality in which the church shares and to which it must respond.

(b) Human and social realities affect theology

One of the results of the recent development in all of these human and social sciences is that today we are able to understand much better than before to what degree our own perspective and condition affect what we see and how we see it. Thanks to psychology we now know something about the manner in which unconscious and subconscious realities affect how we think and feel. Sociology tells us that the way in which we see things also greatly depends on our social, cultural, and other circumstances.

What all this implies is that theologians can no longer speak as if they are disincarnate spirits, but rather have to take into account their own circumstances, as well as those of the church and of humanity at large. The social and human sciences allow us to attain the understanding needed in order to do that.

A characteristic of modernity is its quest for scientific objectivity. Its ideal is an experiment in which all a scientist does is observe what takes place. Postmodernity points out that the scientist has already intervened in the result by the mere process of designing the experiment and deciding what is to be inquired. There is no such thing as a totally objective experiment.

What this implies for theology is that theologians also intervene in what they see and say, and that this intervention has much to do with their cultural, social, and other circumstances. Every reading of Scripture is necessarily an interpretation. The biblical text itself is an interpretation of the experience of the author and of God's people. Since their own interpretations reflect their circumstances, the least that theologians must do is to know and understand those circumstances. Furthermore, since those who listen to a theologian or read theological writings will also do so from their own perspectives, theologians must also understand those perspectives and circumstances of prospective readers or listeners. Therefore, precisely in order to be as faithful as possible, theology must take into account what the social and human sciences tell us about the theologians themselves, about the church, and about society.

To speak of "perspectives" does not mean that we are condemned to total relativity. A way to understand this is to think in terms of a landscape. The landscape is there, it is an object. But each observer sees it from a particular perspective. Any who claim to see the landscape and to describe it with nothing but a general perspective are fooling themselves as well as others. Does this mean that the landscape is not real and objective? Certainly not. But it does mean that the landscape comes to us always through a perspective. Likewise, God's revelation is real and firm, but we always receive it where we are, and we interpret it from where we stand.

Given those realities, if we seek to attain the best possible understanding of the landscape, we must share our own perspectives and experiences with other observers. This has much to do with the communal character of theology, to which we shall return.

5. THEOLOGY AS KNOWLEDGE, AS DISCIPLINE, AND AS WISDOM

There is no doubt that theology involves knowledge. Even in its most rudimentary levels, it requires a certain knowledge of the Bible, of the church, and of human reality. Certainly, we may increase our knowledge in any of these fields. For instance, the knowledge of Scripture may be improved through a study of the original languages in which it was written, so as not to be totally dependent on translations. It is also improved by means of the knowledge of the geography of the biblical lands, of the history of Israel, of the customs and traditions of Semitic and Greco-Roman culture. It is also improved through the knowledge of literary genres and the forms that ancient literature took. The knowledge of the church, although clearly part of the experience of every believer, can also be deepened through the study of church history, of the sociology of religion, and so on. The knowledge of society and its culture(s), which we all have since we all belong to it, is also improved by means of the social sciences that have just been discussed. Also, those sciences help us understand the perspective from which we ourselves read the text—whether we read it from a position of power or of powerlessness.

For all these reasons, theology requires knowledge; but it is more than that. It is important to underline this, precisely because modernity has so underscored the need of knowledge that it has lost sight of other dimensions of theology as discipline and as wisdom.

Theology is a discipline. That word may be used with two different meanings, and both are applicable to theology. On the one hand, a "discipline" is a field of inquiry. Thus we say that geography and mathematics are disciplines. Theology is a discipline in this sense, because it is a field of research with its own methodology. On the other hand, theology is a "discipline" in a second sense, which is at least as important as the first. In this sense, a discipline is a way of life to which we submit in order to reach a goal. Such is the discipline of those who train to compete in the Olympics. In this sense, theology is a discipline because it requires that those who wish to pursue it submit to a discipline. This goes far beyond a program of study—although it certainly includes such a program. Theology is an entire process in which the theologian does not seek only to learn about Scripture and Christian doctrine, but also seeks to be formed by Scripture and doctrine. It is not merely a matter of reading the Bible, for instance, as someone seeking an answer to a puzzle, or a point of information; it is rather a matter of reading the Bible seeking to have it give shape to both life and thought. This is what is meant by claiming that theology is also a sort of wisdom. There is a vast difference between knowledge and wisdom. Knowledge tells us how things are. Wisdom teaches us how to relate to them. Unfortunately, too often theology has so underscored its knowledge dimension that it has forgotten that above all it is to seek and to be a form of wisdom.

This is why late in the Middle Ages, Thomas à Kempis declared that "what we are to seek in Scripture, rather than subtle arguments, is our own benefit," and asked, "What does it avail to reason about the high and secret mysteries of the Trinity, if one offends the Trinity by lacking humility?" In the sixteenth century, reformer Ulrich Zwingli said, "You will know that God is acting within you when you see that God's word renews you, and becomes to you more precious than ever before, when you only listened to human doctrine." What these two authors, and many more, mean by such statements is that what one is to seek in Scripture, and therefore also in theology, is much more than mere knowledge—what the ancients called *scientia*, but also true wisdom—what the ancients called *sapientia*.

Gregory of Nazianzus, already quoted in a different context, declares that theology is not an occupation for everyone, but only for those who are truly committed to it and to its God, for those who "do not turn it into a theme for pleasant conversation, as someone who comments after the races, the theater, or a concert." On the contrary, theology must be the occupation of those who "have been purified in body and soul, or at least are in the process of being purified." This does not mean that theology is the purview of perfect Christians; but it does mean that it must go beyond a mere intellectual entertainment, or the occupation of those who are not convinced that it is a matter of life and death. With words that could very well be applied to much of what today passes for theology, Gregory continues: "Why such earnestness and rivalry in constant speaking? . . . . Why have we tied our hands and armed our tongues? We no longer praise hospitality, nor love of others, . . .

nor do we admire liberality towards the poor, nor nightly vigils, nor tears of repentance. . . . Will the tongue rule no matter at what price? Can you not quell your insatiable speech?" Part of wisdom is precisely in knowing when to speak and when to remain silent, or—as will be said later on—in acknowledging the limits of our own theological undertakings.

6. THEOLOGY AND THE COMMUNITY OF FAITH

Although we often forget it, theology is a function of the church, and not only of specialized theologians or individual Christians. The Christian faith is lived in the community of believers, the church. Likewise, theology must be done in the midst of that community.

Naturally, a theologian will have to set aside significant periods of time to devote to the rather solitary endeavors of study, reflection, and writing. But even during those periods the theologian must remain part of the community of faith. Theology is not a matter of making great individual discoveries, as we see the "mad scientists" doing in horror movies. Its critique of the life and the proclamation of the church is done not from outside the church, but within it, as part of the very community whose faith and life are placed under the light of the Word of God.

Certainly, a theologian will find points in which it will be necessary to call for a reformation in the life and proclamation of the church. However, such a call has value only when it is not an individual matter, but rather finds echo in the faith of the church itself—or at least in a significant sector of it.

It is important to underscore this because modern individualism frequently leads us to imagine that the great theologians have been those who have stood against the entire church, as solitary heroic pillars. The truth is that the great theologians have been those whose work has found echo in the faith and life of the church.

A typical example is the manner in which we imagine Luther and his work. It is true that in the debate of Leipzig, when he was under attack by those who quoted the authority of the Council of Constance, Luther declared that any Christian with the Bible has more authority than all the councils of the church, and that at the Diet of Worms he faced the emperor and his authorities with his famous "Here I Stand." However, this does not make of Luther the solitary hero that sometimes we imagine. What Luther meant at Leipzig was that the authority of the Bible is such that whoever has it has more authority than any council—not for reason of being alone, but rather by reason of being with the Bible. Luther himself staunchly opposed the "false prophets" who soon appeared, each with his own notion of what the Bible said. And what gave him the strength to continue insisting on his doctrine of justification by faith was that such a doctrine found echo in a large segment of the community of faith, which recognized it as being based on biblical authority.

Like Luther, Calvin and the other reformers insisted on the communal nature of the Christian faith, and therefore on the communal nature of theology. Calvin and Luther were both constant students of Christian tradition, and would not depart from it except when forced to do so by their study of Scripture. At a later date, the same was true of John Wesley, who declared that "there is no holiness that is not social." What Wesley meant was that the Christian life is life in community. Likewise, true Christian theology is theology in community.

The fact that theology is done within the community of the church may be carried to such a point that theology loses its freedom in relation to the church, and therefore its critical function. If theology can only repeat what the church already says, it does not have much value. Such a theology may have an apologetic function, presenting the faith to those who do not form part of the community, but it cannot serve as a critique of the life and proclamation of the church.

In extreme cases, such a theology leads to giving such authority to tradition and to the teachings of the church that theology is limited to repeating what has always been said, and cannot even use Scripture to correct the church. Already in the fifth century, Vincent of Lérins declared that only that is to be believed or taught which has been believed "always, everywhere and by all"—*semper, ubique, ad omnibus*. Although Vincent himself qualified this statement, and employed each of the three terms of his formula to clarify and sometimes even to limit the others, in later times the formula itself became a hindrance to theological creativity and inquiry. Even if we set aside for the time being that very little has ever been held with absolute universality, the Vincentian formula can limit theology to the repetition of the past, sacralizes whatever the church declares to be its tradition, and therefore can make it very difficult for theology to critique the life and proclamation of the church in the light of the gospel.

Something similar was declared in the sixteenth century by the Council of Trent, in its effort to refute the insistence of Protestants on the sole authority of Scripture.

However, it is not only among Roman Catholics that this attitude is found. There are also Protestant circles in which, although there is a repeated insistence on the authority of Scriptures, they have to be interpreted in a particular way, and whoever differs in the slightest from such an interpretation is rejected. In such cases, even though we may not notice it, we have allowed ourselves to move to a position very similar to that of Vincent of Lérins—although not nearly as ample and universal as his.

In summary, in the task of theology the relationship between the individual and the community is dialectical or circular: the individual offers a judgment on the proclamation and the life of the church, on the basis of the gospel, but always as a member and participant of that community of faith. The community then acknowledges the correctness or the error in what has been said. On the basis of that acknowledgment, the theologian clarifies, expands, or corrects what was said earlier. And thus the circle moves on.

Furthermore, even after all the long-standing debates about Scripture and tradition between Catholics and Protestants, we must conclude also that the relationship between Scripture and tradition is dialectical or circular. Certainly, the gospel gave rise to the church. It was then the church that recognized the gospel in the books that today form the New Testament, and included them in the canon or list of sacred books. Then, and ever since, the church has had to adjust to that canon as its rule of faith and action. But we always interpret those Scriptures from the perspective of a tradition, which in turn is corrected by Scripture. And thus the circle continues.

7. THE LIMITS OF THEOLOGY

The preceding pages have mentioned some of the dangers that may follow from various ways of understanding or of doing theology. However, the greatest danger that always faces theology is that of ignoring its own limits. Therefore, it is important to point out at least two of them.

(a) Theology and context

The way in which theology most frequently ignores its limits is by forgetting that it always exists within a context, and that from that context it derives a perspective that is always partial, concrete, and provisional. Too often theologians have imagined that what they say does not reflect their own circumstances, and that therefore it is God's own truth. When someone then sees or interprets a particular point of theology from a different perspective, that person seems to be questioning, not what those theologians have said, but God's revelation. But the truth is that every theology has its own perspective, its own historical setting, which lead it to ask certain questions, and that therefore no theology is universal or perennial, that is, equally valid in all places or for all times.

Here again we may think in terms of a landscape, which even though having an existence of its own must always be seen from a perspective. Likewise, whoever did theology in the thirteenth century did it from the perspective of the thirteenth century, and whoever wrote theology in the twentieth century wrote it from the perspective of that time. Neither of the two can claim to have produced a universal theology. Whoever writes theology in the context of the Latino church writes it within that context, and the same is true for whoever writes theology in Europe. The European cannot pretend to speak for all times, places, and people. The male theologian cannot claim that his theology does not reflect his masculine perspective—just as the female theologian cannot claim that her theology does not reflect her own circumstances.

What this means is that *all theology is contextual*, and that any theology that claims not to be contextual deceives itself, and even runs the danger of falling into idolatry by claiming for itself a universal perspective, which only God can have.

This does not mean that each theologian utters only an absolutely individual word. Just as a landscape artist, while having a particular perspective, paints a landscape that exists outside the mind and the taste of the painter, so the theologian speaks of a revelation of God that is there, as a given reality, and that the theologian cannot change at whim.

Even though the discussion of context appears here under the heading of "the limits of theology," in truth, this variety of perspective actually enriches theology. Once theology acknowledges the limits of its own contextuality, it can begin to hear what others are saying from other perspectives, and its own understanding of the gospel is thereby enriched.

Here again the image of a landscape may be useful. Most of us, when we look at a landscape, do so with two eyes. Each of those two eyes sees something slightly different. Our own brain, on the basis of those two perspectives and the differences between them, makes us perceive distances and depth. If we look with a single eye, it is much more difficult to perceive such distances and depth. Therefore, the very fact of having two eyes, and having each of them seeing something slightly different, far from obscuring the landscape for us, or creating confusion, helps us understand that landscape in a way that will never be possible with a single eye.

(b) A human word about God

If it is true that theology speaks of God and the divine purposes, and at the same time remains a human task, it is obvious that its words are always provisional, partial, even precarious. Those who do theology, no matter how much we seek to follow the Word of God—and precisely because we seek to follow it—must recognize the chasm between our words and those of God. To speak about God is to face the Mystery of All Ages. It is like looking at the sun: we risk being blinded. To speak about God is to break forth in praise, and then to be silent in awe. Every theologian would do well to remember the words of Alfred, Lord Tennyson:

> Our little systems have their day;
> They have their day and cease to be;
> They are but broken lights of thee,
> And thou, O Lord, art more than they.
>> "In Memoriam A.H.H."

II. WHO IS GOD?

At the beginning of the first chapter it was pointed out that each discipline or field of study must suit itself to its own purpose and to the object of its study. A significant portion of that chapter was devoted to a discussion of the purpose or purposes of theology, and the various ways in which they may be understood. It is now time to turn to the *subject* or the theme of theology, which is first of all God. Therefore, the two questions to be posed presently are: Who is God? and How do we know God?

Although these two questions are different, they are so entwined that it is impossible to answer them separately, or even in order. Whatever we say about who God is will depend on the manner in which we are able to know God; and whatever we say about the knowledge of God will depend on the manner in which we conceive this God of whom we speak. Therefore, although in the following pages we will be looking at times at one and sometimes at the other of these questions, we shall always be dealing with both.

1. THE KNOWLEDGE OF GOD

How do we know God? In answer to that question, we must begin by asserting that God can only be known when, where, and as God reveals God's self to us. The knowledge of God that we might have always comes from God, and not from ourselves or our own ingenuity. This is what in theological terms is called *divine revelation*.

Traditionally, theologians have distinguished between *natural revelation* and *special revelation*. What this distinction indicates is that there is a certain knowledge of God that may be derived from nature—human nature as well as the physical world—and a certain knowledge of God that comes to us through the biblical tradition, and in particularly through Jesus Christ.

(a) Natural revelation

Throughout the ages, and in various cultures and circumstances, humankind has known that there is another reality above itself, and has seen manifestations of that reality in the wonders of the physical world as well as in the moral order. This is proclaimed by the psalmist: "The heavens are telling the glory of God; and the firmament proclaims his handiwork" (Ps. 19:1). In an entirely different context, the apostle Paul declares that "what can be known about God is plain to them, because God has shown it to them. Ever since the creation of the world his eternal power and divine nature, invisible though they are, have been understood and seen through the things he has made" (Rom. 1:19-20). These texts, as well as the global experience of humanity, affirm that with only contemplating creation, it is possible to know something of the glory of God.

Furthermore, it is not only physical nature that gives us some hint of the existence and character of God, but also human nature. Paul continues his argument affirming this very point: "They show that what the law requires is written on their hearts, to which their own conscience also bears witness; and their conflicting thoughts will accuse or perhaps excuse them" (Rom. 2:15).

In short, whatever divine revelation there is in nature may be seen both in the physical world and in human nature itself.

One must also acknowledge that such revelation of God in nature is neither absolutely clear nor undeniable. One may look at nature and come to the conclusion that it is a cruel order in which the stronger destroy and exploit the weaker, where creatures hunt and eat one another, and where every day there are new deadly microorganisms. Likewise, although our conscience seems to direct us in a path of virtue, the truth is that we can easily rationalize whatever we wish to do, and that there are many people whose conscience does not seem to bother them, or what is even worse, whose conscience seems to justify the most inhumane acts of oppression, exploitation, and cruelty.

There is no doubt that the signs of God in nature can be interpreted in various ways. For instance, many cultures have grounded their polytheistic beliefs in the conflicts and tensions that may be seen in creation. If there is conflict and tension in nature, this is then explained by the conflicts and tensions among the many gods, each of whom governs a portion of nature, but not all of it. Such is the case of the many religions that seek to explain the cycles of fertility by means of myths about the gods. In various parts of the world, diverse people have thought that the reason nature seems to die in winter and revive in spring is that her enemies kill the goddess of fertility, who then rises again every year. In some ancient Indo-American religions, it was thought that periodically the sun bled to death, a victim of his enemies, and in order to renew him it was necessary to revive him by means of blood sacrifices—sometimes human blood.

In summary, the observation of nature may lead to rather divergent religious conclusions, some of which may have nefarious consequences for human life. That is why from very ancient times several peoples—Israel among them—have insisted that in order to know God adequately in nature one needs another key. This key is to be found, not in nature itself, but in history.

(b) Revelation in history

When one reads the Scriptures of Israel, one sees a people convinced that in its history God was revealed. This means that the God of Israel is a God with a purpose. The movement of nature is cyclical: the heavenly bodies go around and appear to come back to their place of origin; the seasons of the year succeed one another in the same order; animals and people are born, mature, reproduce, and die. In contrast, history moves toward something new. There certainly are cycles in history, for empires, like animals and people, also are born, grow, and die. However, those cycles are not a mere repetition of the preceding, but are moving toward a purpose. At least, that is what Scripture tells us. When in Scripture the God of

Israel is identified, this is done not only by God's names—which are several—but also and above all by God's actions in history. God is the god of Abraham, of Isaac, of Jacob, and their descendants (Gen. 32:9; Exod. 3:6, 15-16; 4:5; Matt. 22:32; Mark 12:26; Luke 20:37; Acts 3:13; 7:32). God's own self-identification has to do with God's actions: "I am the LORD your God, who brought you out of the land of Egypt, out of the house of slavery" (Exod. 20:2).

Many students of Scripture have pointed to this contrast between the religion of Israel and that of its neighbors. While those other neighbors worship the baals (or lords) who rule the fields and their fertility, Israel adores the God who brought Abraham and Sarah from Ur, who led the people out of bondage in Egypt, who took them to the promised land, and who later brought them back from exile in Babylon.

There is a great deal of truth in this contrast. However, it must not be carried to an extreme. Certainly, the God of Israel is not only the one who led Israel out of Egypt, but also the one who makes the ground produce grass, and the trees give fruit (Gen. 1:11-12), and who promises: "If you follow my statutes and keep my commandments and observe them faithfully, I will give you your rains in their season, and the land shall yield its produce, and the trees of the field shall yield their fruit" (Lev. 26:3-4). All of this shows that the God of Scripture rules over both nature and history—and therefore is revealed in both.

The revelation of God in history serves Israel—and also Christians—as a key to discern God's revelation in nature. Thanks to what we know of God by the divine actions in history, we can judge the phenomena of nature, and see where and how God is revealed in them.

(In the text just quoted above from Leviticus 26, rain and harvest are connected with the judgment of God upon the people. If the people know the God who took them out of Egypt, they can also see in the harvest the hand of the same God.)

Just as the observation of nature may lead us to widely divergent conclusions, so may the observation of history seem to reveal other gods who are not the God of Israel and of Jesus Christ. It is important to remember this, for otherwise we run the risk of sanctifying and sanctioning everything that takes place in history.

There are many examples of such dangers. Probably the most dramatic is the Holocaust that took place in the twentieth century under Adolf Hitler and his followers. Are we to say that, since God is revealed in history, that horror was a manifestation of the character and will of God? Certainly not! Many other examples could be found in the history of the peoples of the Americas. The arrival of the Europeans brought new diseases and produced injustices and atrocities. Are we to say that, since God is revealed in history, such things were the work of God? Certainly not! The importance of this point goes far beyond theory, for to this day human history is full of injustice, abuse, and exploitation. If all that happens in history is the work of God, the unavoidable conclusion is that God supports the unjust, the abusers, and the exploiters.

This is why in order to see God in history, just as is the case with God's revelation in nature, we need a key that tells us where and how we are to see God acting. The biblical texts behind the last assertion are so many that it is impossible to refer to all of them here. God's self-identification in giving the Ten Commandments is done on the basis of the liberation from Egypt. In the Psalms, there is repeated reference to how God "divided the sea and let them pass through it, and made the waters stand like a heap" (Ps. 78:13), and God's steadfast love is manifested in that God "divided the Red Sea in two . . . and made Israel pass through the midst of it" (Ps. 136:13, 14). Israel uses this key again and again in order to discern the action of God in history. The return from exile in Babylon is interpreted in the light of the liberation from the yoke of Egypt. And the actions of the people must reflect the memory of that great liberating action of God (Deut. 5:15; 16:12; 24:32).

A question that one might ask when speaking of the action and revelation of God in history is whether this happens only in the biblical narrative, or is God also active in the history of the rest of humankind? Before the Spaniards and their missionaries arrived, was God active in the history of the Native American peoples? Although sometimes we tend to think that Israel was an exclusivist people, the truth is that its prophets acknowledged the action of God in the history of other peoples. Thus, Amos 9:7 puts the following words in the mouth of God: "Did I not bring Israel up from the land of Egypt, and the Philistines from Caphtor and the Arameans from Kir?" If there is only one God, that God is concerned not only with the history of Israel—or of the church and Christians—but with the entire history of all of humankind.

This does not necessarily mean that the Philistines, the Arameans, or any other people have known the God in whose hands their history was. The prophet of Israel can declare that his God brought the Philistines from Caphtor, but the Philistines themselves would say that it was their baals who brought them hither. Israel knows that God brought it from Egypt, and therefore can see the action of the same God in the migrations of the Philistines and the Arameans.

However, the fact that the liberation from Egypt provides us with a key that helps us see God's revelation and action in history does not mean that this solves all the ambiguities of human history. When Israel faced the question of whether it should have a king or not, even though they remembered their liberation from Egypt, some thought that the correct answer was yes, and others thought the opposite. Compare 1 Samuel 8:5-22 and 10-19, where a negative judgment is expressed on Israel's desire to have a king, with all that is said in the rest of the Old Testament about the institution of the monarchy.

Therefore, it is possible to say that God is revealed in all of human history, but that in order to see that revelation one has to have the necessary keys—just as in order to understand God's revelation in nature, one has to have a key that nature itself does not provide. At the same time, it is important to remember that even that key does not free us from the ambiguities that are inherent to the human condition, and that people who are completely faithful and sincere can disagree on the manner in which God is acting in their own time.

In any case, just as the liberation from Egypt provides Israel with its key to discern the action of God—a key that retains vital importance for Christians—so does the church have its central key in the person of Jesus Christ.

(c) Revelation in Jesus Christ

Christians affirm that Jesus Christ is the supreme revelation of God. The apostle Paul affirms this by declaring that Jesus is the image of God (2 Cor. 4:14; Col. 1:15). In the Gospel of John, Jesus says that whoever has seen him has seen the Father (John 14:19). What all this indicates is that, just as history is the key to understanding the revelation of God in nature, and just as in the Old Testament the exodus from Egypt is the key to understanding history, Jesus Christ is the key for the entirety of God's revelation.

This in turn implies that any preconceived notions we might have about God must be corrected by what we see in Jesus Christ. If for instance, philosophical arguments lead us to think of a distant

God, quite unconcerned with human reality, when we look at Jesus Christ, God made flesh for love of humankind, we must correct such notions—as was already seen in dealing with philosophy as a means to understand God.

In Jesus Christ we see God made flesh for us, walking in the fields of Galilee with fisherfolk and sinners. We see God healing the sick; feeding the hungry; forgiving sinners; affirming the dignity of women, children, and the alien; speaking harshly about those who believe themselves better than the rest. This is the God in whom Christians believe!

It is important to underscore this, for there are Christians who seem to believe that the best way to glorify God is to insist in the distance between the human and the divine. Certainly, there is an enormous distance and difference between the two. The prophet rightly declares, "For my thoughts are not your thoughts, nor are your ways my ways, says the LORD. For as the heavens are higher than the earth, so are my ways higher than your ways and my thoughts than your thoughts" (Isa. 55:8-9). But that distance is not such that God's love cannot bridge it. Perhaps it would be correct to say that, just as God's ways are much higher than our ways, so is God's love much higher than our love, so that what seems impossible for us is not such for divine love. As will be seen in the chapter on Jesus Christ, the excessive insistence on the distance between God and humanity has made it very difficult for some Christians to accept the notion that in Jesus Christ we truly see God made human. Certainly, God is very different from a human being. Certainly, God is infinitely superior to anything we might imagine. But in spite of that, the best way to know God is to look at a Galilean carpenter, crucified by Roman authority.

(d) Revelation in Scripture

Christians also affirm that God is revealed in the Scriptures of the Old and the New Testaments. Such authority of Scripture has always been the foundation of the life of the church, and in particular of the Protestant churches that resulted from the Reformation of the sixteenth century. Our theology must be grounded on the Bible, and anything that contradicts Scripture must be discarded or at least corrected.

As is well known, the authority of Scripture was one of the pillars of the Protestant Reformation. Since much of what the Protestant leaders affirmed contradicted what seemed to be the tradition of the church, and Roman Catholics defended their own positions on the basis of that tradition, the debate soon focused on the apparent contrast between Scripture and tradition. Among Roman Catholics, the Council of Trent, gathered a few decades after the beginning of the Reformation, declared that both the Bible and tradition are to be employed as a source for the teaching and practice of the church.

Among Protestants, whereas all emphasized the unique authority of Scripture, they did not all agree on the proper place for tradition. Luther, for instance, did not believe that it was necessary to abandon the traditional practices of the church, as long as they did not contradict what was clearly taught in Scripture. Calvin's position was similar, although he felt inclined to reject a number of things that Luther accepted. Among more extreme groups, the notion emerged that in worship the only hymns that could be sung were those taken literally from the Bible, and that no instrument should be used that was not found in Scripture. In such circles, usually only psalms were sung, and normally without any instrumental accompaniment. Instruments such as the organ and the violin, as well as hymns composed by Christians at various times, seemed to them to be part of a tradition that must be rejected in order to be faithful to Scripture.

In contrast to this, the Roman Catholic Church, in its desire to protect tradition from such attacks, began limiting the access of the people to Scripture. This was precisely the time when the printing press began making it possible to distribute *en masse* books that until then were only accessible to persons of significant wealth, or to monastic communities. For fear of the "excesses" of Protestantism, the policy of hindering access to Scripture was followed until the twentieth century, when it was changed, mostly as a result of the Second Vatican Council.

Today it is becoming increasingly apparent that the contrast between Catholics and Protestants on this point is not as sharp as we thought. Among Roman Catholics, Bible study is actively encouraged in unprecedented ways, and many are invited to rethink tradition on the basis of Scripture. Among Protestants, we begin to realize the indissoluble link between Scripture and tradition. Thus we have to acknowledge, in the first place, that it was the church and its tradition that—guided by the Holy Spirit— determined the canon or list of the sacred books; and second, we also have to acknowledge that if the Bible has reached our time, we owe this to many of those ancestors in the faith whose tradition we would earlier have despised.

Let us consider these two points in order. When the early Christians went throughout the world preaching the good news of Jesus Christ, the only Scripture they had was the Hebrew Bible—what today we call the Old

Testament. Then they began writing the books that today are part of our New Testament—first Paul's Letters, then some of the Gospels. At first these books circulated independently one from the other. Then other books appeared that also circulated among the churches—for example, Clement's *First Epistle to the Corinthians*, the *Shepherd of Hermas*, and others. Little by little, the church decided which of these books would be included in the New Testament, and which would not. Therefore, we have to conclude that, although today the tradition of the church must be subject to the guidance of Scripture, at an early time it was that tradition that, led by the Holy Spirit, determined the content of Scripture.

The second point is equally undeniable. The original manuscripts written by the authors of the New Testament have long disappeared. What we have today are copies of copies of copies. Therefore, had it not been for all those Christians who through the centuries devoted themselves to reproducing the sacred text, we would not have the Bible. Also in that sense, no matter how much we insist on basing everything only on the Bible, we are indebted to tradition.

Among Roman Catholics, the years since the Second Vatican Council have seen a great awakening in Bible studies. Not only in schools of theology, but also in thousands of small groups, mostly composed of laypeople and led by laypeople, the Bible is studied as never before. Such study frequently leads people to discover contradictions or differences between the message of the Bible and the practice of the church, and therefore to begin seeking a whole series of reforms in which the Bible is to correct the shortcomings of tradition.

Another point that is very important when we speak of Scripture as the revelation of God is that the Bible was not written to be read by bits, taking a verse from here and another from elsewhere in order to prove a point. The Bible was written in order to guide the people of God in paths of obedience. What is more, almost all the books of the Bible were originally written to be read aloud in the congregation. Although careful and private reading of the Bible is important, it is also important to read the entire text both in private and out loud in the congregation, in order thus to receive its meaning and direction. Another way to say this is that the Bible as God's Word does not simply provide us *information*, but also and above all works for our *formation*—to give us the shape that God wishes us to have both as individuals and as God's people.

Further on in this chapter, under the heading of "The Word of God," more will be said about Scripture as the Word of God.

(e) Faith and reason

An important subject when one speaks about our knowledge of God—a subject that is crucial for the entire theological task—is the relationship between faith and reason, or the place of reason in theology. Since the previous chapter already dealt with the relationship between philosophy and theology, this subject already has been mentioned. However, in order to make things clearer, it is necessary now to return to it, as we discuss our knowledge of God.

There is no doubt that reason has an important place in theology, as it does in every human discipline. Just as it is impossible to practice astronomy without the use of reason, so is it impossible to practice theology without the use of reason. It is reason that makes it possible for us to organize our ideas and words. Without it, we can utter nothing but incoherent sounds. Therefore, whatever we say about God must at least have a rational order.

The ancient Greeks were well aware of this, and therefore the doctrine of the *Logos* became very important for them. This has already been mentioned in the previous chapter, when pointing out how the doctrine of the *Logos* helped Christians such as Justin Martyr claim for their faith any good they found in ancient Greek philosophy. Since the doctrine of the *Logos* is also important for understanding much of what theology has said about the Word of God and about Jesus Christ, it is important to provide some further explanation.

As we reflect on the manner in which we know things it becomes apparent that such knowledge requires some measure of commonality between the order of things and the order of our thought. Our thought tells us that two and two are four. If we then take two apples and join them to two other apples, we have four apples. How do we explain this strange fact that what our mind tells us is confirmed in reality? The explanation of the ancient Greeks—and the most common explanation throughout the history of philosophy—is that the order of things coincides with the order of reason. In other words, there is a common "reason" or order between our mind and reality external to us. That order or rationality in the universe is what the ancient Greeks called the *Logos*. If our mind can understand the universe, this is because in both our mind and in that universe there is order, rationality, *Logos*.

This is why the ancient Greeks affirmed that all knowledge comes through the *Logos*. That is also why Justin and other Christians were able to employ the philosophers' doctrine of *Logos* in order to claim whatever they found in philosophy that could be useful for their theological task.

It is important to recognize and acknowledge the limits of reason when it comes to the knowledge of God. One must ask, for instance, if a God who has to fit the molds of our reason can in truth be the sovereign God, or is merely one more idol.

Unfortunately, too often theologians and philosophers have believed that in fact God has to fit such molds; that God has to be exactly as our reason conceives the divine; that therefore it is possible to deduct, from what we know of God by means of rational argument, how God must act.

In the last chapter, mention was made of Zanchi and many others who tried to prove the doctrine of predestination on the basis of God's omniscience and omnipotence. As was stated then, the grave error in such arguments is in imagining that we truly understand what we mean by God's omniscience, and therefore making such omniscience fit the very limited mold in which we can conceive it.

Both the value and the limits of the use of reason in the theological task can be seen clearly when considering the proofs that have traditionally been offered in order to demonstrate that God exists. Let us therefore turn to a brief consideration of those proofs.

2. THE PROOFS OF GOD'S EXISTENCE

Is it possible to demonstrate that God exists, and to do this in such a way that the conclusion is absolutely undeniable? Furthermore, once we have proved the existence of God, will this God whose existence reason demonstrates be the same as the sovereign and loving God of Christian faith? In the history of Christian thought, there have been attempts to prove the existence of God following two different paths: (a) on the basis of the created world and (b) on the basis of reason itself.

The decision to take one of these two paths depends on how we understand and explain knowledge itself. At various times and places, there have been those who have affirmed that the surest knowledge is that which comes to us through the senses, and others who have insisted that the surest knowledge is precisely the one that is absolutely independent of the senses. Today, some would say "seeing is believing," while others would say that the best knowledge is that which is not seen, but which is known directly by the mind, such as purely mathematical knowledge. The first seek knowledge that is based on the senses, and which the senses can test; the latter seek knowledge that does not depend on the senses, which after all can deceive us. The first group will seek to prove the existence of God on the basis of the created world; the other, on the basis of thought itself, hoping to come to conclusions that cannot be denied no matter how the senses might deceive us.

(a) Proofs on the basis of the created world

These are the most common and the most easily understood proofs of the existence of God. In their simplest expression, they are based on the argument that the existence of the world proves the existence of its creator. One of its most famous expressions claims that if a traveler in the middle of a desert finds a watch it is logical to conclude that someone else has been there before. Since the universe is much more complex than any watch, it is logical to think that someone has made it. In other versions of the same argument, one examines the complexity of the world—of atoms, molecules, genetic codes, heavenly bodies, and so forth—and concludes that such complexity can only have been created and ordered by a higher mind, that is, by God.

The classic expression of this sort of argument is the "five ways" of Saint Thomas Aquinas. As a philosopher, Saint Thomas was convinced that the best knowledge is that which comes to us through the senses, and therefore all of his five ways begin with the existence of the created world, just as our senses manifest it to us, in order then to prove the existence of God. Briefly stated, these "five ways"—which in reality are simply different forms of the same argument—are: (1) *On the basis of movement*: All that moves is moved by someone. This requires the existence of a "prime unmoved mover," that is, of a being who is the origin of all movement. (2) *On the basis of the order of causes*: Everything has a cause. This requires the existence of a being who is the ultimate cause of all things. (3) *On the basis of the contingency of beings*: All the beings in the world are contingent (that is, they could very well not exist). What is it, then, that makes them exist? The answer must be a necessary being, that is, one who exists by its own nature, and not out of an exterior causation. That being is God. (4) *On the basis of the degrees of perfection*: There are in the universe some things that are "better" than others. This requires the existence of a perfect being who is the measure of all goodness and perfection. (5) *On the basis of the end of things*: Everything in the world shows itself to be moving toward an end. That is the reason there is order in the universe, since it is precisely in moving toward that end that there is order. This requires the existence of such an ultimate end. That end is God.

(b) Proofs on the basis of pure reason

All proofs under this other heading seek to demonstrate the existence of God in such a way that, even were the world not to exist, one could not possibly doubt the existence of God. In other words, they seek to show that the existence of God is an absolute necessity of reason itself—just as two and two will always be four, no matter whether or not there are things to be counted. Just as mathematics can show that the very idea of a triangle requires that its three corners add up to 180 degrees, so do these proofs try to show that the very idea of God implies existence—that to speak of a nonexistent God makes as much sense as to speak of a triangle with four corners.

The classic expression of this sort of proof is Anselm's "ontological argument." Anselm had already written another book in which he tried to prove the existence of God on the basis of the created world. But he was convinced that true knowledge is purely rational knowledge, that which does not depend on whatever the senses might tell us. Since the existence of the world itself is a datum of the senses, to prove the existence of God on the basis of the existence of the world does not constitute an absolutely undeniable proof. Therefore, in a second work Anselm tells us that he asked God to illumine him so that he could discover such a proof, and the result was his famous "ontological argument."

Anselm begins by defining who or what is this God whose existence he wants to prove, and declares that God is the most perfect being that can be conceived—or, in his own words, "a being such, that it is impossible to conceive another greater than it." Thus, the question is whether such a perfect being exists. Anselm's answer is that it has to exist, for the idea itself of perfection includes existence. Just as it is impossible to conceive of a triangle with four corners, so is it impossible to conceive that the "most perfect being that can be thought of" does not exist, for in that case it would be less perfect than all the things that do exist.

Although other authors have offered other arguments along these lines, they all have this point in common: they try to prove the existence of God as an absolute requirement of reason itself.

(c) The value and the limits of such proofs

There is no doubt that these proofs have served to open the way to faith for many people. People who thought that it was illogical to believe in God have been moved by these proofs, and as a consequence have opened themselves to Christian witness and proclamation in a way that would have been very difficult for them without these proofs.

There are two important limits to all of these proofs. The first is that they can all be refuted. Whoever does not wish to be convinced by them can offer counterarguments.

For example, the argument that all that exists must have a cause, and that therefore God is the first cause of all things, can easily be refuted by asking why one does not apply to God the same principle, asking what is the cause of God. If the world must have a cause because everything must have one, then God too must have a cause. In other words, if the world is a sequence of causes and effects, in such a way that everything that exists and everything that happens must have a cause, and each of those causes must in turn have its own cause, and so on successively, how do we know that the long chain of cause and effect really ends somewhere—that is, in God—and does not simply continue into infinity?

Likewise, the purely logical argument, which claims that the very idea of a perfect being implies its existence, can be refuted in various ways. The most common is to say that existence is not an attribute of the essence of a thing. As soon as Anselm published his argument, there was a monk who answered that it is possible to conceive of a perfect island, but this does not mean that such an island must exist.

The second shortcoming of all these arguments is that, even if they do prove the existence of something, they do not necessarily prove that such a being is the God of Christian faith.

If we prove that there is a First Cause of all that exists, it still remains to be shown that such a Cause is the same being whose existence we affirm when we say that we believe in God. There could conceivably be a First Cause or a Supreme Being without one necessarily having to conclude that such a being is to be conceived as does the Christian faith.

Thus, what is true of all the rational and philosophical arguments that theology could employ is also true in the specific case of the proofs of the existence of God: in the best of cases, they open the way to Christian faith, but they do not necessarily lead to it. Perhaps they help some unbelievers overcome some of the obstacles that would not allow them to believe. However, if such people remain at the level of these arguments they will still not know the One whom Scripture calls "the living God."

3. THE WORD OF GOD

God can only be known through God's Word. This is simply a restatement of what has been said before, that in order to know God there must be a revelation from God. A fundamental principle of the manner in which the Hebrew-Christian tradition understands God is that God speaks, that there is a Word of God. There are some important points to be underscored about this Word of God.

(a) The Word is creative action

In speaking about the Word of God, the first point to be clearly understood is that in Scripture the Word of God is much more than the manner in which God communicates with us. For us today, a "word" is simply an expression or a sound by which ideas that are in our minds are transmitted to the mind of another person. If I say "horse" whoever hears me thinks about a horse. But the Word of God, even though it does let us know God, is much more than that. The Word of God is creative. The Word is God's creative power. When God speaks, what God utters springs into existence.

This is seen in Scripture as early as Genesis, when God creates by speaking: "God said, 'Let there be light'; and there was light" (Gen. 1:3; compare with verses 6, 9, 11, 14, 20, 24). The same is also asserted in the Gospel According to John, where it is said about the Word of God that "all things came into being through him, and without him not one thing came into being" (John 1:3). This is the meaning of the promise: "For as the rain and the snow come down from heaven, and do not return there until they have watered the earth . . . so shall my word be that goes out from my mouth; it shall not return to me empty, but it shall accomplish that which I purpose, and succeed in the thing for which I sent it" (Isa. 55:10-11).

It is important always to remember this, for what God does upon speaking is not just telling us something, but also transforming our reality. When we truly hear the Word of God, not only do we learn something, but we also become something new.

This is closely related with what was said before—that the purpose of Scripture is not only to inform us, but also and above all to form us. It is also related to what was said about theology, whose purpose is not only that we know more about God, but also and above all that we may be more obedient to God's will.

(b) The Word is God

The beginning of the Gospel of John, which has just been quoted, not only asserts that all has been created by the Word of God, but also that the Word is God: "In the beginning was the Word, and the Word was with God, and the Word was God" (John 1:1).

The reason why the Word of God does much more than provide us with information is that strictly speaking the Word is God. The Word is God creating, calling, redeeming. When we truly encounter the Word of God, we encounter God, and not just words or information *about* God.

According to John, the place where we most clearly and directly meet that Word is in Jesus Christ, because "the Word became flesh and lived among us" (John 1:14). That is why it was asserted above that Jesus Christ is the supreme revelation of God.

This leads us to two other crucial subjects. The first is the relationship between the Word and God the Father. John says that the Word was God, but also that the Word was *with* God. How are we to affirm both things? The second is how we are to understand the affirmation that "the Word became flesh." The first of these matters will be discussed later on in this chapter, when speaking of the triune God. The second issue will be studied in the chapter about Jesus Christ.

(c) The Bible as Word of God

These questions imply that it is necessary to clarify what we mean when we say that the Bible is "Word of God." In the Bible itself, as has just been stated, the Word is above all God speaking and acting. The Bible is not God, and therefore it must be Word of God in a different sense and a different manner. The Bible is Word of God because it is the instrument that God uses to speak to us and to transform us—remember once again that the Word of God not only says, but also does, and that the Bible not only informs, but also forms. What makes the Bible be Word of God is not its paper and ink, but the Holy Spirit of God, which acts in such a way that in the Bible we encounter God.

Some theologians, such as Karl Barth, have tried to express this point saying that the Bible *is not* Word of God, but rather *becomes* Word of God by divine action. Since some people may be confused or scandalized by such an assertion that the Bible is not the Word of God, it is necessary to clarify what it means. What is meant by this assertion is that a closed Bible is not strictly speaking Word of God, for it neither speaks nor acts. (In a discussion some years ago with a very conservative professor, a student asked if when someone hits another with a Bible is the other person actually being hit by the Word of God. The answer is obviously that such is not the case.) But the point goes further than that. It also means that it is possible to read the Bible and be so closed to the action of the Holy Spirit that one does not hear the Word of God. On the positive side, it means that when the Holy Spirit makes the Bible become Word of God for us we are in the presence, not only of inspired words or of good teaching for life, but of God!

The Bible is Word of God because through the action of the Holy Spirit it leads us to the Word of God, Jesus Christ. And the Bible is Word of God because through the action of the same Spirit the words of the book transform us, so that we become a "new self, which is being renewed in knowledge according to the image of its creator" (Col. 3:10).

4. THE TRIUNE GOD

In the previous section, commenting on the first verse of the Gospel of John, the question was posed of how and why it is possible to say both that the Word "was God" and that the Word "was with God." Also, in the same section there were repeated references to the Holy Spirit, who is God, but is not the Word of God. This leads us to the doctrine of the triune God, which is fundamental in Christian theology.

From the very beginnings of Christianity, there are formulas or phrases that refer to the triune nature of God. Paul uses phrases such as "the grace of the Lord Jesus Christ, the love of God, and the communion of the Holy Spirit" (2 Cor. 13:13). In other places in the New Testament, one finds similar formulas. We are told that believers "have been chosen and destined by God the Father and sanctified by the Spirit to be obedient to Jesus Christ and to be sprinkled with his blood" (1 Pet. 1:2).

(In all these quotes, it is important to remember that the title of "Lord" that Paul gives to Jesus Christ was the title employed in the Greek version of the Old Testament that Paul used—the Septuagint—in order to refer to God. Therefore, when Jesus is called "Lord," he is being equated with the God of the Old Testament.)

These formulas reflect what has been the experience of believers through the ages. We believe that Jesus Christ is Lord, that he is God, and that we ought to worship him as such. We know that the Holy Spirit is God, and we worship the Spirit also as God. At the same time, in the Gospels Jesus speaks of God as being both one with him (John 10:30) and other than him (John 5:17, 30, 36). Jesus Christ, while being God, is also the way that leads to God (John 14:6). And we know that the Holy Spirit leads to Jesus.

All of this is expressed in the doctrine of the Trinity, which affirms that Father, Son, and Holy Spirit are three, but are a single God. Given the difficulties involved in such paradoxical affirmation, throughout the history of Christianity there have been various attempts to resolve them by eliminating one or another of the poles of the paradox—saying, for instance, that only the Father is God in the strict sense, or that the three are not really distinct. Such "solutions," although seemingly simple, were rejected by the majority of Christians because they denied some important aspect of what the trinitarian doctrine affirms—it is for that reason that they were usually called "heresies." Since it was in response to such heresies or facile solutions that trinitarian doctrine developed, the best way to understand that doctrine is to begin by considering such attempted solutions.

The use of the term "Father" for the First Person of the Trinity, and of "Son" for the Second Person, has a long history in Christian theology. These must not be understood as affirming any sort of masculinity in God, but rather of asserting a relationship in which there is a single source, from which the Second Person derives its being. Other traditional terms, although not used as frequently, are *Source, Word,* and *Holy Spirit.*

Most of these facile solutions regarding the Trinity can be classified in two groups or basic positions: *subordinationism* and *modalism.*

(a) Subordinationism

This proposed solution tries to solve the difficulties by affirming that the Son and the Spirit are inferior—subordinate—to the Father. Very simply expressed, what the various subordinationist theories propose is that the Son and the Holy Spirit are divine, but not in the same way or to the same degree in which the Father is divine. Although throughout history there has been a wide variety of subordinationist doctrines, the one that may serve as a model for the rest is Arianism.

Arianism derives its name from Arius, a theologian in the fourth century who proposed it. Like most subordinationist theologians, Arius began from that understanding of God that we have already encountered in other chapters, which sees God as distant from the world, a pure being with the purity of the inaccessible. For Arius, the essential characteristic of divinity is immutability. God cannot change nor vary in the least. However, in the world everything changes; life is change; history is change. How, then, can the immutable God relate with the mutable world? Arius's answer is that the Word or Son of God is an intermediary being between God and the world. The Word is not eternal like God, but is rather a creature that God made as the instrument through which to create the rest of the world. The Word is not immutable as only God is, but mutable. (It may be helpful to point out here that this does not really solve the problem posed, for Arius never explains, if it is true that the immutable cannot relate with the mutable and therefore needs a bridge, how the Word, being itself mutable, can relate to the immutable God.)

Regarding the Holy Spirit, although Arius himself did not say much, later his followers declared that the Spirit must also be a subordinate being, and not strictly speaking divine.

It was against such doctrines that the Nicene Creed was formulated, as a way of rejecting them. That creed affirms that the Son is "begotten, not made"—that is to say, is not a creature, as Arius claimed—and that he is "of the substance of the Father"—that the Son shares in the same divinity as the Father.

(b) Modalism

This other position seeks to solve the problems inherent in the doctrine of the Trinity by declaring that the Father, the Son, and the Holy Spirit are only three faces or "modes" in which God is made manifest—hence the name "modalism."

The most common form of this doctrine—which is relatively common in many churches to this day—suggests that God is Father in the Old Testament, Son in the New, and now Holy Spirit. Such formula certainly safeguards the unity of God, but is not faithful to the biblical witness, where, for example, the Holy Spirit appears both in the Old and the New Testaments, and where Jesus refers to the Father as other than himself. Furthermore, such a doctrine does not keep the distinction between Father, Son, and Holy Spirit, but reduces these to names or roles that God takes up at various circumstances. In some of its contemporary forms, modalism speaks of God as Creator in the Old Testament, Savior in the New, and now as Spirit.

(c) The doctrine of the Trinity

The classical expression of the trinitarian doctrine is that in God there is "one substance and three persons." Although such a formula does not appear anywhere in Scripture, its purpose is to affirm what the Bible seems to say on the matter: that the Father, the Son, and the Holy Spirit are three—they are not the same—but they are a single God. This doctrine affirms that the Father is God, and that the Son is no less divine than the Father—and the same regarding the Spirit. However, it also holds that the three are a single God. Certainly, this does not solve the difficulties posed above. But at least it acknowledges the limits of our understanding, and does not seek to force God to fit within those limits. What all of this means is that trinitarian doctrine and its classical expression—three persons, one substance—are not descriptions of God, but rather signposts along the way to let us know where the pitfalls are that we must avoid: *tritheism* (believing that there are three Gods), *subordinationism* (believing that the Son and/or the Holy Spirit, while being divine, are not fully such) and *modalism* (believing that "Father, Son, and Holy Spirit" are no more than three names that we give to three modalities in which God appears). The doctrine of the Trinity, without claiming to explain how these are to be reconciled, reminds us that it is important for us to affirm that God is only one, while at the same time we confess that the Father is not the Son, nor is the Son the Holy Spirit.

Such a trinitarian doctrine has been depicted by means of the following graphic:

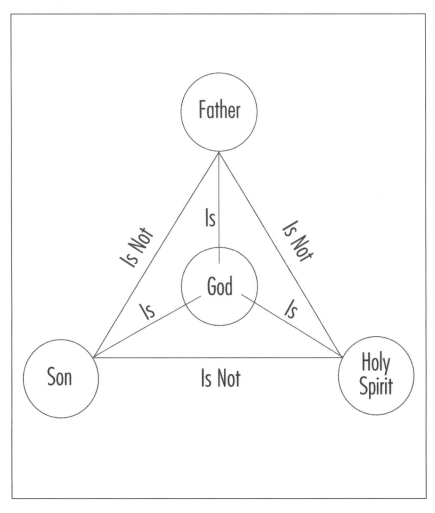

(d) The Trinity as a model for believers

Perhaps the best way to approach the doctrine of the Trinity is by not trying to explain it, but rather by seeking to imitate it. What this doctrine affirms is that Father, Son, and Holy Spirit share a single divinity, and that they share in such a way that none of the three is thereby impoverished. Likewise, within the Trinity, while there are distinctions, there is also equality. Such is the nature of God's life and God's love. And, if such is the love and the life of God, ours must imitate it. Our mutual love must lead us to seek equality and to share knowing that, as in the case of the Trinity, such sharing, far from impoverishing, enriches us.

III. WHAT IS THE WORLD? WHO ARE WE?

Did God create the world and its inhabitants? If so, how and to what end? How do we humans relate with that creation and with God? And, if God did create all that exists, why is it then that there is so much evil and so much suffering in creation?

This chapter will consider the doctrine of creation in the light of these questions. A brief summary of the controversies in the early church that led it to affirm the doctrine of creation, particularly by including it in its creeds, will help us understand why the church thought that this doctrine was important, and who it was who denied it or seemed to threaten it. Also, we must consider how the development of new scientific and critical methods of research has led to different ways of responding to these ancient and perennial questions about the origin of the universe and the purpose of our own existence.

1. THE DOCTRINE OF CREATION

From its very birth, the Christian church has affirmed its belief in God as creator of the world and all its inhabitants. The ancient Scriptures, which the church took from the Hebrew tradition—what we now call the Old Testament—begin by affirming the creative activity of God, which stands at the basis of all that exists. The Scriptures produced by the church and in its early years—what we

55

now call the New Testament—show that the apostles and the primitive Christian community reaffirmed belief in God as creator (Matt. 10:6; Acts 17:24-26; Rom. 1:25; 2 Cor. 5:5; Heb. 3:4; 1 Pet. 4:19; Rev. 14:7). The same is affirmed by the most ancient Christian writers, the early creeds and councils, and the hymns and other worship elements that have been preserved. Perhaps the best known among us is the "Apostles' Creed," which many churches recite every Sunday, and which begins by declaring: "I believe in God the Father Almighty, maker of heaven and earth."

(a) The challenge of heresies

If the ancient church reaffirmed the doctrine of creation so insistently, it was because there were those who denied it, and the church was convinced that this doctrine was essential for Christian faith.

The doctrine of creation was not simply something that the church had inherited from Hebrew tradition, but was also of crucial importance for the Christian faith, something that should be affirmed against any who would deny or distort it. Therefore, the repeated reaffirmation of creation in the ancient creeds was not due simply to the logical sequence of ideas from creation to consummation, but rather to the conviction of many in the church that if one did not understand and affirm the doctrine of creation this would in turn lead to the denial of several other essential doctrines, as well as to practices that were not compatible with Christianity. Not all people who joined the church believed or had been taught at home that creation was good, and that it was the work of the one God revealed in Jesus Christ. Many brought with themselves all sorts of beliefs about the origins of the world and of humanity, and about their value and purpose—beliefs derived from various philosophical traditions or from the old religions that they had previously followed. Such people joined the church in worship, but it soon became apparent that their belief differed from what Scripture taught, for they did not really believe that the physical world was good, or that the human body was good. For such people, everything material was evil, or in the best of cases had nothing to do with God and the divine purposes of salvation. They were ready to affirm that the human spirit, which is not material and which according to them comes directly from God, is good; but they could not say the same regarding the body. In consequence, only the spirit or the human soul had the capability of returning to God.

Platonism left a profound imprint on the faith and beliefs of many Christians regarding the origin, value, and purpose of the world. From its beginnings in the fourth century before Christ, the Platonic tradition had affirmed that this world was not the creation of the Supreme Being, but of a secondary intermediary or "demiurge," and that the material world was an imperfect copy of a higher world of pure ideas. That which we see is no more than an image or an imperfect reflection of the eternal and perfect "forms" or "ideas" of that other world. The human spirit must find a way to ascend to that purely spiritual world, and therefore the value of the material world depends on its ability to reflect those perfect and eternal forms. According to Plato and a very ancient tradition, the body was the tomb or prison of the soul, which could only be freed through the contemplation of eternal realities.

Although the church rejected such doctrines because they contradicted the Christian view of creation, in various ways and under various disguises they have often reappeared in the Christian community, and echoes of them can be found even among some of the most respected Christian writers, both of ancient times and of the present.

Another movement that also denied the doctrine of creation, and which made inroads in the Christian church, was called *Gnosticism*, because its followers claimed to have a special *gnosis* or knowledge, which had supposedly been revealed secretly to them or to some apostle to whom they attributed the origin of their doctrines. The Gnostics, like the Platonists, believed that only the spiritual has true value, and that the human spirit, trapped within this physical, earthly, and evil body, yearns to return to the heavenly home from whence it proceeds. Only those who have the illumination of the secret *gnosis*, and therefore know what they in truth are, will be able to flee from the bonds of this physical world, and thus attain salvation.

Although Gnosticism took many forms, it generally held that the spirit of the true Gnostic—the one who had the *gnosis* or sacred illumination that leads to salvation—was actually a portion or a spark of divine spiritual reality trapped in a material body. For some reason, which each Gnostic school explained in its own way, these eternal spirits, part of the spiritual reality of another world, have fallen from their spiritual world and are now trapped in a physical body and polluted by the material world. In this world, which some called an "abortion" of spiritual reality, the spirits of the Gnostics slumber amid the rest of humanity, until they receive the message sent from on high by means of a specially designated messenger. Among Christian Gnostics, it was claimed that this purely celestial and spiritual messenger was "Jesus" or "Christ," who came to awaken the Gnostics from their slumber and to show them the way to return to the spiritual world. The rest of humanity, those who do not have within themselves the spark of eternity, have no hope of salvation.

Another threat to the doctrine of creation came from Marcion, whose doctrines were similar to some that are heard even today in some churches. Marcion, who founded a church to rival that of the rest of Christians, held that there are two gods. One of them is the god of the Old Testament—Yahweh— and the other is the supreme God, the Father of Jesus Christ. Yahweh is a vengeful and perhaps even ignorant god, who created this world with all its imperfections and placed us in it. The supreme God, the Father of Jesus Christ, by contrast, is a loving and forgiving God, who would never have created this material world, since matter is inferior and even evil. Therefore, all that has to do with the body, including procreation, is evil and polluted, and must be avoided until the merciful God of Jesus Christ frees us from this prison in which Yahweh has placed us. Naturally, since matter is evil, Jesus did not come in a physical body nor was he born from Mary, but rather appeared already as a mature man with a body that only had an appearance of matter. And he certainly could not have really suffered or died.

It goes without saying that the church rejected such doctrines, which denied not only creation, but also the continuity between the two Testaments, and even the incarnation of God in Jesus Christ—to which we shall return in the next chapter.

From its very early days, and as soon as it was challenged by them, the church rejected all the various doctrines that denied the creation of the world by God—doctrines such as those from the Platonic tradition, those of Gnosticism, and those of Marcion and his followers. This does not mean, however, that such doctrines entirely disappeared.

Although it would seem that Gnosticism was only a problem for the church during the first centuries of its history, the truth is that its impact—as well as that of spiritualizing Platonic tendencies— continues to this day. That is why one often hears sermons on the evil of the material world, or the restlessness of the soul within the body, and believers are called to flee from this world and its matter, and to seek the higher spiritual world. Sometimes we are told of the need to nourish the soul, because in the last analysis, that is all that is important and it is all that really matters to God. Some preachers harp on the theme that the material world will perish and only the spiritual will remain. Just as the early Gnostics held that the world and the body were the result of an evil deed or an error on the part of some heavenly spiritual being, there are Christians who believe that human physical existence is the result of sin and the "Fall"—which will be discussed later on in this chapter. Furthermore, in recent decades there has even been a revival of

Gnosticism, so that Gnostic groups appear everywhere—especially among those who follow the "New Age spirituality." One even begins to see groups called "Gnostic societies," which mix a number of the traditional Gnostic teachings with elements taken from other religions and from the occult. Significantly, almost all of these new religions deny the doctrine of creation—or at least diminish it to a secondary doctrine, for all that is important is the spiritual life.

(b) The response of the church in the creeds

One of the manners in which the church responded to all of these errors, and reaffirmed the doctrine of creation, was by including it in its creeds. This may be seen in the two best known and most generally employed to this day, the Apostles' Creed and the Nicene Creed.

The creed that we usually call "Apostles' Creed" was not composed by the apostles, as was affirmed by later tradition. It was a creed that began circulating in Rome about the year 150, and which in the ninth century became commonly used in the Western church.

The Nicene Creed was promulgated by the Council of Nicaea in 325 (this was the first ecumenical council, that is to say, a council of the whole church), and then the Council of Constantinople (in 381) made some additions to it. It is more generally accepted than the Apostles' Creed, for it is employed both in the Western churches—Catholic and Protestant—and in the Eastern ones— the Greek, Russian, Ethiopian, and so on.

Creeds—both the Apostles' and the Nicene—were employed in baptism, so that the person who was being baptized had to affirm them. Therefore, in classes preparing people for baptism the creed that they would have to affirm was taught and discussed. After the baptism, the repetition of the creed in worship reminded people of what they had learned while preparing to be baptized. Therefore, the words of the creed made a profound impact in the formation and the faith of believers.

Both the Apostles' Creed and the Nicene speak of God as "almighty." The Greek word translated as "almighty" is *pantokrator*, and in truth means, not that God is able to do anything and everything, but rather that all things are under God's rule.

The word *pantocrator* comes from the same Greek roots that we find in *Pan*-American and in demo*cracy*. The first of these roots means "all," and the second means "government." Thus, the *pantocrator* is the ruler of all.

Both creeds emphasize the scope of God's power by declaring (the Apostles') that God is "maker of heaven and earth" and (the Nicene) that God is "maker of heaven and earth, and of all things visible and invisible." The lordship of God is not limited to celestial and invisible realities, as some Gnostics claimed, but embraces all: heaven and earth, the visible and the invisible.

The church stressed this doctrine in its creed, not by mere whim, or simply to cause controversy, but rather because it was convinced that the doctrine of creation was fundamental for Christian faith. God is creator and sustainer of all that exists—for the doctrine of creation does not refer only to the origin of things, but also to their present subsistence. It is to this creation of his that Jesus came (John 1:11), and what he took was true flesh from this creation. It was in that flesh that he lived his life, that he died, and rose again. It is in this creation, as a part of it, that we subsist by God's grace—as the whole of creation also subsists. Unfortunately, too often Christians have forgotten the essence of this doctrine, and have been carried away by escapist doctrines, as if the world were not God's good creation, or as if God were creator only of heaven and of things invisible. Furthermore, as will be seen later on, these mistaken interpretations of our relationship with the world have led many either to seek to sever their relationship with nature, or to abuse it.

2. CREATION AND SCIENCE

Debates among Christians about the creation of the world and its inhabitants did not end with the formulation of the ancient creeds. Even when one affirms that God is "maker of heaven and earth, and of all things visible and invisible," this may be interpreted in various ways.

In the thirteenth century, there was a debate about whether God had made all things "out of nothing" or out of a preexistent matter. It was a time when Western Christianity had just rediscovered some ancient writings of Aristotle, many of them having arrived through the mediation of Muslim Spanish philosopher Averros, in which it was claimed that the primordial matter of the universe was eternal. Since Aristotelianism arrived together with a great scientific advance, it became the highest science of the time, and there were theologians who declared that God had made the world from such an eternal matter. Rejecting such a position, other theologians such as Bonaventura and Saint Thomas Aquinas insisted that matter also is created by God. What was at stake was whether there existed another eternal principle besides God, or rather God was the origin of everything, as the ancient creeds affirmed. At the end, it became customary to claim that creation is *ex nihilo*—out of nothing—as a way of insisting on God as the only creating principle of all things.

In relatively recent times, the development of new scientific methods has posed new challenges to the traditional understanding of creation. This is particularly true of the theory of evolution.

This theory was initially proposed by Charles Darwin, who held that species evolved according to the principle of "the survival of the fittest." Those species that exist today have evolved from others that existed before, so that it is possible to find common ancestors—many of them extinct—among various existing species. (Although this theory has provoked bitter controversies, and there are Christians who believe that it is satanic, it is important to remember that Darwin himself was a devout Christian and a promoter and supporter of missions.)

Almost as soon as this theory was published, there were Christians who saw it as a denial of creation as it is described in the first chapters of Genesis. This has led once again to the matter of the relationship between faith and science: Are they compatible? Is it possible to reconcile the data of science with the tenets of faith? Can science support and enrich faith, or only question and negate it? Given such questions, there is an undeniable reality: the church cannot ignore the challenges posed by the new scientific methods and their discoveries.

These questions are not new, for they have been posed repeatedly throughout history. Another famous case had to do with the theories of Copernicus and later of Galileo, about the movement of the heavenly bodies. Until then, it was commonly held that the Sun revolved around the earth. When Copernicus and Galileo proposed a different vision, there were ecclesiastical authorities that condemned their theories, on the basis that Joshua had stopped the course of the Sun (Josh. 10:12-13). Likewise, some insisted that the earth could not be a sphere, for the Bible speaks of "the ends of the earth," and a sphere has no end.

On these matters, Christian opinions vary enormously. Some seek to reconcile evolutionist theories with Scripture, claiming that the six days of creation are metaphoric, and that they each refer to a stage in the process of creation. Others insist that there is no conflict, once one understands that the important subject of Genesis is not how God made the world, but that all that exists is God's creation, and that God upholds all things in existence. In such a case, whether God made the world in six days, or by means of an evolutive process that took millions and millions of years, is of secondary importance. Others hold that the stories in Genesis 1 and 2 are to be taken literally, and that God did make the world in six days. According to the latter, the very authority of Scripture is threatened when one accepts any description of the origin of things different from that of Genesis—be it the theory of evolution or the big bang theory of the origin of the universe. Once such authority is doubted, such people claim, what keeps us from ignoring all that the Bible says, including the advent, death, and resurrection of Jesus Christ?

It is necessary to point out that those who defend a "literal" interpretation of Genesis are not defending such an interpretation, but rather a compilation and selection from two different stories whose details are mutually exclusive and which cannot therefore be interpreted literally without falling into contradiction. Whereas in Genesis 1:20-27 God creates first all the animals, and finally the human being, male and female at once, in Genesis 2:15-22 God creates first the man, then the animals, and finally, from the man's rib, the woman. This would seem to strengthen the claim that Genesis does not try to tell us exactly how God has made the universe, but simply that all things that exist are God's creation.

As a means of reconciling science with the doctrine of creation, some claim that creation has to do with the origin of things, and science with their actual functioning. What is then suggested is that God in the beginning created the world, and set it in motion as one sets in motion a machine. From there on, the world functioned according to its own laws, and it is these laws that science studies.

This was the position of the Deists. Deism, which began in England and reached its high point during the seventeenth and eighteenth centuries, was an attempt to reduce religion to its basic, universal, and rational elements. According to the Deists, such elements in religion are innate to the human mind, where they have been placed by God, and it is possible to know them without any special revelation whatsoever. They are: belief in the existence of God, the obligation to worship God, the requirement of a devout and virtuous life as part of that worship, repentance for sin, and a final reward or punishment for our actions. According to the Deists, all religions, including Christianity, have left aside the simplicity and reasonableness of natural religion. That is why most Deists rejected the notion of a special divine revelation, or of divine interventions in the course of nature, and insisted that their proofs for the existence of God were purely rational. As part of this system, it was then said that God did create the world, but no longer intervenes in it, but rather allows it to function according to the rational physical laws to which God subjected it.

Although this position was held, among others, by some Christians who thought that they were showing that in its essence Christianity is eminently rational, most Christians saw in such theories a serious threat to their faith. For example, if God does not intervene in the world, why does Scripture tell us that we should bring our petitions to God? Only so that we might be consoled, even though nothing will change? What about that important theme in the Bible, that God acts in history? Does the God not exist who does wonders? How can we relate to a God who is not in the least bit interested in us, and for whom we are no more than cogs in a huge machine?

This takes us to the central point of the conflict between science and religion in the last two or three centuries. During that period, science has looked upon the world as a great machine, subject to fixed and predictable laws—just as the functioning of an automobile can be foretold on the basis of a series of mathematical formulas. The universe is then conceived as a closed entity, in which nothing from outside can intervene. Contrasting with that vision, Christian faith has traditionally seen the world as an open entity: open first in the sense that both its origin and its purpose come from God, from the creator God who is the Alpha and the Omega, beginning and end, of all things. Open also in the sense that this God does intervene in the universe, and therefore there is indeed reason to pray and to hope for a better world. Fortunately, in more recent decades theoreticians of physical sciences have begun to critique the traditional scientific vision of the universe as a mechanical and closed entity. Therefore, it is to be hoped that in the future the conflicts between science and religion will be lesser—or at least that they will follow a different course.

Although it is true that Christian faith cannot accept the vision of a closed world, it certainly does accept the vision of an orderly world. God is not only the creator of all things, but also their sustainer. The doctrine of creation does not mean only that God made the world and set it in motion, but also that God keeps it and sustains it in existence. Therefore, the laws of nature that science studies—for instance, the law of gravity—are part of the creating and sustaining action of God. The world of Christian faith is not a capricious world, but rather one that follows laws created and established by the God, maker of "all things visible and invisible."

3. THE HUMAN CREATURE

The doctrine of creation does not refer only to the origins of all that exists, but also has to do with how we relate with the rest of creation. The relevance of this should be obvious, for today more than ever we are becoming aware of the damage humanity has done and can do to the environment. However, before turning to our responsibility toward creation, it is necessary to consider our place within that creation.

(a) Human beings are part of creation

In Genesis 2:7 we are told that "the LORD God formed man from the dust of the ground, and breathed into his nostrils the breath of life; and the man became a living being." According to the Bible, humankind has been made "from the dust of the ground," that is to say, the very substance on which we tread, which we cultivate, and which we contaminate. Later on in the narrative, when the man and the woman have sinned and they must face the consequences, that close relationship between the human and the earth is reaffirmed when God tells Adam: "Cursed is the ground because of you" (Gen. 3:17). And finally, also as a consequence of sin, that which was dirt or earth will return to its original condition: "You are dust, and to dust you shall return" (Gen. 3:19).

The very name "Adam," which the man is given in Genesis, is a play on words that indicates his origin from earth, for in Hebrew *adham* means human being (and it is thus used repeatedly in the Old Testament, to refer, not to an individual, but to humanity), while *adhamah* means earth.

These passages have often been used merely to underscore how ephemeral human life is. Dust we are, and to dust we shall return. But there is throughout this story of creation another dimension that is crucial if we are to understand correctly our relationship with the rest of the world that God has created. It is not only a matter of our being made from the dust of the earth, but also of all the animals being made of the same earth (Gen. 2:19). We are kin to all of creation, for it as well as we are made of "dirt"—or, as we would say today, of atomic particles.

Furthermore, according to that story in Genesis 2, all animals were created in order to provide companionship for the human creature, since the reason God makes them is that "it is not good for the man to be alone" (Gen. 2:18). And, as we are told in Genesis 1:26, this human creature will have dominion over the rest of creation—which will be discussed further on.

The story in Genesis 2 that tells of man being created first, then the animals, and finally the woman, has been interpreted as affirming that the woman's purpose in life is to be a "helper" to the man, who is to be her lord. Such an interpretation has no basis on the text. There, God seeks to create an appropriate helper for the man. The word that here is translated as "helper" normally is employed in Hebrew Scriptures to refer to God as Israel's "helper." What is translated as "adequate," "appropriate," or "comparable" literally means "as in front of him," and is applied to an image in a mirror. Unfortunately, the old King James Version translated that word as "meet," meaning "fitting," and later by joining the words "help" and "meet" the new word was invented, "helpmeet." On the notion of "helpmeet" society then poured all its preconceived ideas about the relationship between a man and a woman. That is not at all what is meant here. The animals are not proper companions for the man, precisely because they are not like him. Instead of being the man's companion, they must be subject to him. That is why he gives them names, since the act of naming is an act of claiming dominion or control. But when God finally creates the woman, and the man sees that she is like him, for she is flesh of his flesh and bone of his bones, rather than giving her a name, he simply shares his with her, although in a feminine form (Gen. 3:20). Therefore, the relationship of dominion and control between male and female among humans is not part of original creation, but is rather the result of sin—as is also affirmed in Genesis 3:16.

Sadly and tragically, an incorrect interpretation of this passage has been and still is an excuse for much abuse against women. It is time for Christians— male as well as female—to reject such an interpretation, and seek to do justice to all who carry in them the image and likeness of God.

(b) The human being is different from the rest of creation

Although the book of Genesis affirms that the human creature is made of the same stuff as the rest of creation, it also affirms that it is a special creature. This is apparent in the two narratives of Genesis 1 and 2.

In Genesis 1, after calling the rest of creation into existence, and as a final touch, God creates humankind. God says: "Let us make humankind in our image, according to our likeness; and let them have dominion over the fish of the sea, and over the birds of the air, and over the cattle, and over all the wild animals of the earth, and over every creeping thing that creeps upon the earth." And then the narrator adds: "So God created humankind in his image, in the image of God he created them; male and female he created them" (Gen. 1:26-27).

In Genesis 2, God creates first the man, decides that it is not good for the man to be alone, and then creates the rest of the animals in order to keep him company. In the end, since none of the animals measures up to this task, God creates the woman, whom the man acknowledges as his equal: "This at last is bone of my bones and flesh of my flesh" (Gen. 2:23).

From these two texts it is apparent that that which distinguishes the human creature from the rest of creation is, first of all, the "dominion" given to it—to which we shall return; and, second, being made in the "image and likeness" of God.

The subject of the "image of God"—*imago dei*—in the human creature has been the subject of many and very different interpretations.

In some cases, this passage has been interpreted in the sense that there is a physical likeness between the human creature and God—that is to say, that God actually looks like us. (Some have also claimed that this goes beyond a physical similitude, for they distinguish between the "image" and the "likeness" and then claim that, while one is physical or material, the other is spiritual or rational.) Clearly, this leads to an unacceptable anthropomorphism. As a reaction to this, some have argued that the image of God in humans is in their reason: God is the rational being *par excellence*, absolute Reason, and we are copies or reflections of that Reason. Others have argued that the image is in free will, or in the ability that the human creature has to transcend itself—to see itself "from outside."

Leaving aside all these various interpretations, there are at least three points that must be underlined: the first is that there is a clear relationship between the "image" and the "dominion." This has important consequences, as will be seen when dealing with our responsibility in creation. Second, it is necessary to underscore that, no matter how one interprets the *imago dei*, the very presence of that image implies that every human being with whom we relate carries that image, and to devalue, oppress, or destroy a human being is to devalue, oppress, or destroy the very image of God. Third, it is important to note that in this text both the man and the woman have been created after the image and likeness of God, and that therefore the woman's dignity is the same as the man's.

(c) The recurrence of the Gnostic error

A common interpretation of Genesis 2:17 claims that the human being is a composite of earth and divine spirit—or of physical matter and spiritual divinity. We are then told that our sinfulness is the result of our being made of earth, and that the reason we are not content with the present physical life, but seek more, is that in truth there is something divine in us.

Such an interpretation has no foundation in the biblical text, but comes rather from the widespread tendencies to think that the physical is evil and the spiritual good, as did the ancient Gnostics. In the biblical text, being made out of earth is part of the good creation of God, who has made all the other animals out of the same earth. The divine breath that turns the human into a living being does not mean that God has infused part of the divine essence into the human creature, but simply that breath, life, is a gift of God.

There has been much discussion as to whether human beings consist of two parts, namely body and soul, or of three—body, soul, and spirit. The first position is usually called the "dichotomist"; the other is the "trichotomist." The debate is ancient, and already in the ninth century the Fourth Council of Constantinople (869–870) responded to the debate by rejecting trichotomism. Both positions can claim support in the New Testament. Matthew 10:28, for instance, seems to support the dichotomist position, whereas 1 Thessalonians 5:23 speaks of "spirit, soul, and body." What is more, there are in the New Testament a number of passages that seem to continue the Hebrew tradition, which saw the human being as a single indivisible entity (see Matt. 20:28; John 10:11). Such an apparent discrepancy would seem to indicate that for the biblical authors this was not an important issue. What was important was not to know how many parts there were to the human being, but rather how to lead lives that were pleasant to the sight of God. That the church of the New Testament did not seek to clarify this matter is an indication that its interest was more a matter of curiosity than of obedience. The Bible is not interested in telling us how we are constituted, but rather in the reason for which we have been created.

Once again, part of this discussion is grounded on the semi-Gnostic tendency of some Christians, seeking to separate the body and the soul, as if the only important aspect of a human being were the soul, and the body were no more than a transitory dwelling for the soul.

This has many practical consequences, some of which will appear elsewhere in this chapter. One that often goes unnoticed is that this discussion tends to imply that intellectual life has greater value than physical life. The practical outcome of this is that those whose tasks have to do with intellectual work and management consider themselves to be worthier than those whose tasks have to do with the physical subsistence of the body and of society— farmers, workers, and trash collectors, for example. Also, precisely because it is thought that such occupations are inferior, society tends to set them aside for those whom it considers inferior, be it because of the color of their skin, their sex, their culture, or any other reason.

On the basis of such an erroneous interpretation of the biblical text, one frequently hears sermons where we are told that the physical body is evil, or at least that it is of no great consequence, for at the end it is mere dust, which will return to dust. Even worse, sometimes such sermons tell us that our spirit is actually divine, and that therefore we are to be concerned only about it, and not about the body in which it is imprisoned. As has already been stated, such doctrines are not Christian in origin, but rather Gnostic, and do not reflect the biblical witness.

It is important to correct these errors, not only because they contradict Christian doctrine, but also because they lead to mistaken

relationships with the world and with others. A proper understanding of creation serves as the basis for a proper relationship
with the world and with others.

4. THE HUMAN CREATURE IS A SINNER

Even though we affirm that creation is the work of God, it is
obvious that creation is not as good as it ought to be. Everywhere
we see suffering, death, and injustice. The Bible and Christian tradition interpret this paradox in terms of sin, beginning with what
traditionally has been called the "Fall."

(a) The Fall

In the Genesis narrative, immediately after the two stories of creation in the first two chapters, we come to the tragedy of chapter 3.
There, the innocent, pleasurable, and even idyllic existence that has
just been described is interrupted when Adam and Eve disobey
God and eat of the forbidden fruit.

The most common way of interpreting the story of the first temptation is that
Adam and Eve allowed themselves to be carried away by ambition when the
serpent promised that they would be "like God." In that case, pride is at the
very root of evil. It is thus that the passage has been interpreted since the times
of Saint Augustine. But in the ancient church, as may be seen in the writings
of Irenaeus, there were other ways of understanding that original temptation.
According to the biblical narrative, Adam and Eve were already like God,
who had made them after the divine image and likeness. Therefore, sin is not
in ambition, but rather in the lack of faith, in not believing what was already
a reality, that they were "like God." These two interpretations have practical
consequences, for if pride is the root of sin, then the poor and the oppressed
should not aspire to more than they already have or to more than they already
are. If the root of sin is in forgetting the image of God in us, then the same
people must demand respect and justice precisely because, like every other
human being, they are "like God."

The consequences of that act of disobedience are disastrous, and
result in a series of situations that are not part of God's purpose in
creation. The woman suffers in childbirth, and is made subject to

her husband. The man has to sweat and to struggle against nature, which is now refractory, for even the earth itself is cursed as a result of human sin, and produces thorns and thistles. Very soon fratricide will appear, as well as a myriad of other evils. It is thus that the Bible affirms what daily experience confirms: that evil is real, that it is powerful, that it corrupts God's good creation. Between creation as it is originally willed by God and creation as it exists stands sin.

The question of the origin of evil has puzzled and perturbed philosophical minds for centuries. The problem is in the difficulty in affirming three points that seem to be mutually contradictory: (1) God is good; (2) God is all-powerful; (3) evil is real. Every solution that has been proposed throughout history simply ignores or minimizes one of these three points. Atheists use the existence of evil in order to deny the existence of a good and powerful God. Christian Science denies the existence of evil, attributing it to our imagination. So also, in a more sophisticated way, do the philosophers who claim that what appears evil from our perspective is not really such from the divine perspective. Some limit God's power claiming that God had to create free human beings, and that this required the possibility of sin.

Even though it would be very pleasant and edifying to claim the opposite, the truth is that the Bible does not offer a solution to this problem. If we say that the explanation lies in the human being, who introduced sin into creation, there still remains the question of the serpent and its origin. If we claim, as has sometimes been said by Christian tradition, that the serpent is Lucifer, who is a fallen angel, all that we have done is postpone the question, for one must still ask why God did not simply make angels who could not fall. Thus, what the Bible offers is not an explanation of the origin of evil so as to satisfy our intellectual curiosity, but rather an affirmation that evil is real, and that it draws us as well as all of creation away from the divine purposes.

That neither philosophers nor theologians nor even the Bible itself offer a satisfactory explanation of evil should not surprise us. What makes evil such is precisely that it interrupts the order, that it breaks all harmony, that it has neither reason nor explanation. Were we able to explain it, it would no longer be the powerful and overwhelming mystery of iniquity that it is.

(b) The scope and power of sin

What is clear from the foregoing is that sin stands between the purpose of creation and its present reality. Perhaps that shall suffice to give us some idea of the scope and power of sin. However, perhaps as a consequence of sin itself, we humans are constantly finding ways to make it appear that sin has less power than it does.

In the Bible, the scope of sin is universal. When a woman is brought to Jesus so that he may judge her and he declares, "Let anyone among you who is without sin be the first to throw a stone at her" (John 8:7), no one dares to do so, for all must acknowledge their sin. Paul declares that "all die in Adam" (1 Cor. 15:22), that "sin came into the world through one man" (Rom. 5:12), and that all have sinned, and therefore have fallen short of the glory of God (Rom. 3:23). This universal scope of sin is what is usually meant by "original sin." Since Paul relates it to Adam, much of Western theology has understood original sin in terms of an inheritance. Thus it is common to speak of "the sin that we have inherited from our ancestors." However, there are other understandings of original sin.

One of the main problems with the understanding of original sin as an inheritance is that too often it has led Christians to think that the act of procreation in itself is sinful, since it transmits sin to a new generation. Augustine declared that, since it is impossible to have sexual relationships without concupiscence, it is in such a concupiscent act that sin is transmitted to children.

In any case, this understanding of original sin is not the only one that existed in the ancient church. Already toward the end of the second century, Clement of Alexandria claimed that the sin of Adam was only a symbol of the fact that we all eventually would sin. Similar opinions have appeared throughout history, and more recently in the various liberal theologies of the nineteenth and twentieth centuries, which affirmed that all sin on their own account. This interpretation avoids the notion that sin is simply inherited, as one inherits physical traits. It does not seem to take into account the full scope and power of sin, which does not depend only on our actions, but goes far beyond our own freedom and our decisions.

Roughly at the same time as Clement, Irenaeus spoke of the universality of sin as a result of human solidarity. The human race is one, much as a single body whose head is Adam. Therefore, in Adam's sin, literally we all have sinned, just as in a body the actions and decisions of the head also are the actions and decisions of the body. (This is related with the manner in which Irenaeus sees the saving work of Christ, as the new head of a new body of salvation.)

No matter which of these views one takes, the important point is that sin is universal, that no one can escape its power, and that we are bound by it from the very moment we come into existence.

Furthermore, sin is such that it corrupts the entire human being. Sin is not just an action or a series of actions, but a condition, a way of being, a slavery from which we cannot free ourselves. Whoever sees sin only as an evil action, apart from the very condition in which one lives, does not really understand its full power.

Among ancient Christian writers, it was Saint Augustine who most underscored this point. He held that the power of sin is such that, even though Adam and Eve were free both to sin and not to sin, the fallen and unredeemed human being only has freedom to sin. This does not mean that such a person has no freedom. At each step in life there is ample freedom to choose among a multitude of alternatives. Some of these may be preferable to others, but they are all sinful! A helpful analogy would be to say that we all have freedom to move about as we please, but not to fly. Since we do not have freedom to fly, we are still free, but only to walk on the earth. Likewise, the fallen human creature has freedom, but only to sin. According to Augustine, such unredeemed humankind is a "mass of perdition."

For Augustine, as later for Calvin and many others, this implies that humans do not have the freedom to decide on their own redemption. In order to accept the offer of salvation, we need the grace of God, which takes the initiative in the process of conversion. Such teachings have given rise to strong and bitter controversies within the church, for the apparently inevitable conclusion is that only those are saved on whom the grace of God takes such initiative, and that if some are damned, this must be because God grants grace to some and not to others—which leads to the doctrine of predestination.

These teachings of Augustine are the basis on which Calvin and the entire strict Calvinist tradition affirm, not only that salvation is by God's grace—as all Christians affirm—but also the "total depravity" of humankind and the doctrine of predestination. This doctrine had also been affirmed by Augustine, Luther, and many others, but it eventually came to be a particular trait of orthodox Calvinism.

There is another way in which Christians diminish the power of sin—or rather, do not realize how much power it has, which actually makes them more susceptible to it. This is by turning sin into a spiritual and private matter, something between God and the individual. Thus, it is sin to lie, to blaspheme, to commit adultery, and so forth, but we then ignore the structural dimensions of sin, which go far beyond such actions that we may commit. Certainly, in the Bible, not only sin against God is condemned—idolatry, blasphemy, and so on—but also sin against the neighbor—such as injustice and oppression. But even beyond such acts, sin lies also in the very structures that promote and produce them. Sin is an entire order of things, an entire system of organizing—or disorganizing—God's creation. This is what the Bible calls "principalities and powers."

Paul affirms that in the cross Christ "disarmed the rulers and authorities and made a public example of them" (Col. 2:15). And in Ephesians 6:12 we read that "our struggle is not against enemies of blood and flesh, but against the rulers, against the authorities, against the cosmic powers of this present darkness, against the spiritual forces of evil in the heavenly places." This theme of the structural character of sin was taken up during the nineteenth century, and on into the twentieth, by the proponents of the Social Gospel in order to point out that many of the problems of society are not because of those who suffer their consequences—the poor, the unemployed, for example—but rather to sinful structures. Thus, if there is unemployment, the reason for this is not that people are lazy, but rather that the economic system produces and sometimes even requires unemployment. Something similar was done late in the twentieth century by the various theologies of liberation, which named and condemned the social structures that produce oppression and suffering.

5. OUR RESPONSIBILITY AS GOD'S CREATURES

As has been repeatedly stated, the doctrine of creation is not limited to the origin of things, but actually has significant implications for our practical life, both in our relationships with the world around us and in our mutual relationships.

(a) Our responsibility toward the rest of creation

In recent decades, and increasingly as the years go by, we are becoming aware of the damage perpetrated by humanity on the rest of creation. Every year animal and vegetable species disappear that will never again be seen over the face of the earth, and much of this is a result of the pollution of the environment and the destruction of the natural habitats of such species—forests, wetlands, and rivers. In many of our cities the air is so polluted that breathing the air is unhealthy. There are strong indications that the excessive and constant use of fossil fuels is producing atmospheric and climatological changes such as the warming of the earth and the growth of deserts. All of this, and much more, we learn from both science and from the press.

However, knowledge is not enough to motivate us to act wisely or appropriately. Significantly, it is precisely the countries that are more technologically advanced and where, therefore, there is greater knowledge of the damage that pollution causes, that such pollution is greatest. Even Christians, who claim that creation is God's work, are part of that very process, and are quite ready to injure creation in exchange for a bit more comfort.

Sadly, it is precisely in the traditionally "Christian" countries, or where at least Christians have been most numerous for a longer time, that many of the products, machineries, and procedures that most pollute the environment have been developed and produced. Even more tragic is that it is possible to draw a line of continuity between a certain understanding of creation and these dire consequences. It was indeed on the basis of the biblical text that claims that humankind is to have dominion over creation (Gen. 1:26) that Western civilization felt justified in its attempt to control creation by means of technology. In its quest for such dominion, that civilization colonized and destroyed others, and to this day no one knows the consequences that its actions may eventually have for the environment and all of creation.

According to that interpretation, when God gave humans dominion over the rest of creation, we were given *carte blanche* so that we could do with creation whatever seemed best or most convenient to us. Therefore, if a mountain stands in the way of my plans for development, I simply level it. If a forest has good wood, I have the absolute right to cut it down. If a river is a convenient sewer where I can dispose of the chemical waste produced by my industry, that is precisely why God has put it there, and I was placed there in order to have dominion over it.

What we forget in such cases is that the dominion that God gives the human creature in Genesis is dominion in the image and likeness of God. God's dominion over humanity and over creation is not capricious, exploitative, or selfish, but rather dominion in love.

It is a dominion in such love that eventually God becomes flesh in order to suffer on the cross!

If, as the biblical witness repeatedly asserts, we are "stewards" or administrators in God's name, our dominion over creation must be part of that stewardship. If we have power over nature, that power has been given so that we may use it to the benefit of all of creation, and not according to our whim or convenience.

Such is the Christian doctrine of creation and our place within it. Since it does not suffice to believe such things, they must be worked out in practice, James rightly reminds us that "faith apart from works is barren" (James 2:20). Perhaps the first work incumbent on those of us who study theology, who preach and who teach, is to remind the church that its faith in the God, creator of heaven and earth, demands that we be committed to loving that creation as those who truly believe that it is God's.

(b) Our responsibility toward others

Even though others are also part of creation, our responsibility toward them merits separate attention. This is important because we usually find it easier to claim that we are creatures of God, made after the divine image and likeness, than to remember that the same is true of the rest of humankind—including those whom we do not like or those who do us evil.

Therefore, the first thing to be said regarding our responsibility toward other human creatures is that we have to show toward them the same respect that we must show toward the rest of God's creation, and that this does not depend on their political or social standing, their nationality, their religion, their race, or any other such thing, but is simply grounded on the fact that they are God's creatures.

Second, we have to remember that the divine image and likeness—*imago dei*—discussed above is found in every human creature. Whoever tramples another, tramples that image. Whoever honors another, honors that image and the God who stands behind it.

Third, since the "dominion" is equally given to all human beings, and since this is dominion over the rest of creation, and not over other human creatures, this implies that no one has the right to make use of such dominion to the detriment of others, and certainly that no one has the right to exercise dominion over another.

This is why an ancient preacher at a time when slavery was still legal, said to slave owners "You are subjecting under the yoke of servitude someone who was created to be master of the earth, whose creator made so that he might have dominion. Apparently you wish to overturn what God has ordained. You forget that your dominion is limited to irrational creation" (Gregory of Nyssa, Homily 4).

In summary, God is the creator of all things, which therefore are good. Among these things created by God, the human creature has a special place, because it bears the image and likeness of God. However, this does not mean that humans have the right to exploit nature as they wish, but exactly the opposite: it means that we are responsible before God for whatever we do with nature or with another.

That we do not see this constantly practiced in our daily lives is one more sign of the power of sin, which interposes itself between creation and God's purposes for it.

In Scripture, sin is an evil of such magnitude that it cannot be counteracted by merely human means. In the Hebrew Scriptures, the answer to sin is love and obedience to God, and hope in the final triumph of that God of love. In the New Testament, God becomes the answer by taking flesh in Jesus Christ and inviting humanity to a new beginning. This is the subject of the next chapter.

IV. WHO IS JESUS CHRIST?

There is no doubt that the center of the Christian faith is the person of Jesus Christ, from whom it takes the very name of "Christianity." However, who is this Jesus Christ whom we call Lord and Savior? And, since we call him "Savior," how is it that he saves us? These are the two classical questions that theology has posed under the heading that is usually called "Christology"—that is to say, the doctrine about Christ. The first question, Who is Jesus Christ? is usually called the question of the "person" of Christ, whereas the second, about how it is that he saves us, is the question of his "work." Therefore, the first part of the present chapter will be organized under two headings: the person and the work of Jesus.

1. THE PERSON OF JESUS

The basic source for all that we may say about the person of Jesus is the New Testament, to which we then add our own experience of faith—both individually and as a church—and finally the issues posed when the church began to think through that faith. It is best, then, to begin with a very quick overview of what the New Testament says about Jesus.

(a) Jesus in the New Testament

In the brief space allowed here it is impossible even to review all that the New Testament says about Jesus. However, it is possible to underline some important points that are the foundation of what later christological doctrine seeks to express.

1. First, it is clear that the New Testament presents us a Jesus who is much more than a human being, no matter how special. This is already seen in the first chapter of John, where we are told that the Word was in the beginning with God, that the Word was God, and that this Word was made flesh in Jesus. Matthew and Luke affirm that Jesus was born of a virgin, which indicates that his very existence is not the mere result of human history and activity, but of a direct intervention from God. Matthew also underscores his authority when in the Sermon on the Mount Jesus repeatedly says, "You have heard that it was said to those of ancient times . . . but I say to you . . ." What has been said in ancient times was spoken by God; and now Jesus, claiming divine authority, dares to add to the ancient words of God's Law. In several passages in the New Testament, Jesus claims a special relationship with God, whom he calls "Father," and he even asserts that "the Father and I are one" (John 10:30). Paul calls him "Lord," which was the manner in which the Old Testament spoke of God. (Most of the quotations from the Hebrew Scriptures in the New Testament—and all of Paul's quotations—do not come directly from the Hebrew text, but rather from the the Septuagint. In the Septuagint, God is usually called "the Lord.")

All of this indicates that in the New Testament Jesus is presented as much more than a human being, an extremely wise teacher, or a particularly saintly person. Jesus is no less than the Word of God made flesh, the Lord who created all that exists. Jesus is divine.

2. In the New Testament, Jesus is not presented as an alien messenger, but rather as one who came "to his own" (John 1:11), and whose coming was prepared through a long time. Part of the purpose of the genealogies that appear at the beginning of Matthew and Luke is precisely to affirm this. Matthew begins his genealogy with Abraham, indicating that throughout the history of the people of Israel God was preparing the advent of Jesus. Luke begins much further back, with Adam, thus claiming that such preparation dates from the very beginning of creation.

This must be seen in connection with what was said in the previous chapter about creation, that the Gnostics and Marcion believed that the God who sent Jesus Christ was not the same one who had made this world and who had been revealed to Israel. On the basis of such belief, the same people denied that God had been preparing history for the advent of Jesus. On the contrary, until that advent all history was under the reign of evil, and Jesus came into it as an alien messenger, and not as someone who comes "to his own."

3. The Jesus of the New Testament, no matter how divine, is still human. Jesus is born small and unable to fend for himself (Luke 2:7). Then he grows in strength and in wisdom (Luke 2:40). At various points in the Gospel narrative he is tempted, he is hungry and thirsty, he eats and drinks, weeps, perspires, suffers, and dies.

4. The humanity of Jesus does not deny or diminish his divinity—indeed, the two are not even opposed. The Jesus of the New Testament is one, divine and human. His words and his actions are both human and divine at once.

5. The Jesus of the New Testament is both victim and conqueror. Throughout the process of the passion, people carry him to and fro, they spit on him and insult him, and eventually kill him. But Jesus rises again from among the dead, a conqueror, not only of those who killed him, but even of death itself. These two elements—death and resurrection—are so entwined that both are victorious, so that Jesus triumphs in the cross (Col. 2:15). Furthermore, at the fullness of time, the New Testament expects that Jesus will come again in glory and judgment (Matt. 25:31-32).

All of these are essential elements of what would slowly develop into the Christology of the church: Jesus is divine and human, and this divinity and humanity are so united that it is impossible to separate them.

(b) Jesus in the experience of faith

The witness of the New Testament did not remain as dead letter or pure history. What the New Testament says came out of, and found expression in, the worship and the life of Christians. One of the most ancient writings in which a nonbeliever refers to Christian faith and practice declares that they gathered the first day of the week and that, among other things, they would sing "hymns to Christ as to God." At the same time, in the same service the "memoirs of the apostles"—that is, the Gospels—were read, and these constantly reminded believers that this one whom they worshiped as God was also human. The experience of faith of Christians through the generations has kept hold of these two realities, and has seen in their paradoxical juxtaposition the very core of its faith.

It is important to remember this, because the christological controversies that will necessarily engage our attention in this chapter may appear as mere unnecessary speculation unless we remember that those who took part in them were seeking for ways to express and understand their faith in the Jesus of the New Testament, both divine and human.

(c) The development of christological doctrine

From an early date, most Christians rejected the extreme positions of those who claimed either that Jesus was a mere human being or that he was purely divine or heavenly.

On the one extreme, Gnostics, precisely because they considered the body and all of physical creation evil, usually denied that Jesus had really taken on human flesh. His body was not really such, but rather an appearance. This doctrine is usually called "Docetism," from a Greek root that means "to appear." For docetic Gnostics, Jesus was a purely divine spirit, and his humanity was only apparent.

At the other extreme, there were some who held that Jesus was a great teacher, and no more. Some claimed that his obedience was such that God adopted him as a son, although he was not this by nature. This theory is usually called "adoptionism."

Over against both extremes, the church categorically affirmed that Jesus is both divine and human. Such an affirmation, however, did not explain how such union of the divine and human was possible.

Furthermore, such union of divinity and humanity in Jesus Christ was even more difficult to understand because an ever-increasing number of theologians had come to the point of defining divinity in such terms that its union with humanity seemed to be a contradiction. This was due in part to the impact of philosophy on theology when, as was already explained in the second chapter, theologians began seeking points of contact between Platonic philosophy and Christian doctrine. In that process of establishing relationships and parallelisms, they came to conceive of God in terms of the traditional attributes of perfection in Greek philosophy, such as impassibility and immutability, which understood the perfection of the Supreme Being in contrast with the imperfection of all that is passing and human. Being immutable is a necessary characteristic of God, whereas to be human means being mutable. Once the matter is posed in this manner, it was to be expected that the incarnation of God in Jesus would seem to be a great contradiction.

There were two main tendencies among those who sought to explain or to describe the Incarnation. On the one hand, those of the tendency usually called "Antiochene"—because its intellectual center was in the city of Antioch—feared that the humanity of Jesus Christ might be denied or diminished. This became a more real threat to them when someone from the opposite tendency claimed that humanity and divinity in Jesus were like a drop of vinegar in the ocean: although the vinegar is still there, the immensity of the sea is such that one sees and tastes nothing but pure sea. For the Antiochenes, this was tantamount to declaring that Jesus was not truly human. Therefore, in order to safeguard the humanity of Jesus, the Antiochenes were inclined to establish a clear distinction between the divine and the human in the Savior—thus resulting in what theologians call a "disjunctive" Christology.

The most famous and controversial of Antiochene teachers was Nestorius, who as Patriarch of Constantinople preached a series of Christmas sermons in which he declared that one should not affirm that Mary bore God, but rather that she bore Christ. According to Nestorius and his followers, in Christ there are "two natures and two persons": a human nature and person, and another that is divine. These two are joined, not as a single reality, but rather through a "voluntary union"—that is, that both desire the same. (At least, it is thus that Nestorius has generally been interpreted, even though there are many fine points of his doctrine on which historians do not agree with one another.) Although modern-day Protestants may have the impression that the sermons that Nestorius preached and the opposition to them were a matter of Mariology, what actually was at stake was not the honor or the titles due to Mary, but rather in what sense Christ is God. If it is not correct to say that God was born of Mary, then one cannot say either that God walked in Galilee, or that God hung on a cross. And, if such is not the case, what is the particular meaning or value of the Incarnation and the cross? It was because of these considerations—as well as a series of complex political circumstances—that the Third Ecumenical Council, gathered at Ephesus in 431, rejected the teachings of Nestorius and affirmed that Mary is "Mother of God"—literally, "bearer of God."

The other tendency, usually called "Alexandrine"—because its intellectual center was in Alexandria—feared that, if too clear a distinction was made between divinity and humanity in Jesus, the unity of the two would be lost. Since this unity is at the very heart of the Christian faith, this caused the Alexandrines grave concern. For this reason they insisted on such unity, thus producing what theologians called a "unitive" Christology—contrasting with the "disjunctive" Christology of the Antiochenes. For this tendency, what is of paramount importance is the union of divinity and humanity in Jesus, even if in order to affirm such union one has to sacrifice something of his full humanity.

One of the first Alexandrine teachers to follow this line of thought was Apollinaris, who declared that Jesus was physically human just as any one of us, but that in his case the Word of God occupied the place of the human mind. Even though such a teaching may be quite common in some churches today, it contradicts what the New Testament tells us of Jesus, who is human not only because he has a human body, but also because he is tempted, suffers, and weeps as other human beings would. In any case, the teachings of Apollinaris were rejected by the Second Ecumenical Council, gathered in Constantinople in 381.

Other persons of similar tendency then suggested what was already mentioned above, namely, that the humanity of Jesus is joined to his divinity as a drop of vinegar is joined to the sea: Jesus is certainly human, but that humanity is eclipsed by the glory and the immensity of his divinity. Therefore, although it is correct to say that Jesus is "of two natures"—as the sea and the ocean are "of two natures"—one should not claim that Jesus exists "in two natures," because the human has been absorbed by the divine. Since in Greek the word *physis* means "nature," those who held this doctrine were dubbed "Monophysites." This position was rejected by the Fourth Ecumenical Council, gathered in Chalcedon in 451, again because it seemed to contradict the biblical picture of Jesus, and also because if the humanity actually disappeared in the divinity, the Incarnation becomes irrelevant.

Finally, in the Council of Chalcedon, in the year 451, a middle ground was agreed upon. Although this did not solve the question, at least it served to delineate the limits for future debates. According to the *Definition of Faith* of Chalcedon there are in Christ "two natures in one person." What this means, in brief, is that Jesus is one, that he cannot be divided between the human and the divine, and that he is equally and fully both. To this day, this is the official position of most Christian churches—the Roman Catholic, the various Protestant churches, and Orthodox churches in Greece and Russia.

There is in the region of Iran and Iraq, as well as in India, a fairly small church that is usually called "Nestorian," because it holds doctrines that are similar to those attributed to Nestorius. There are others that are often called "Monophysite," because they reject the decisions of Chalcedon, even though their doctrine is often very similar to that of Orthodox churches. The largest of these churches are in Egypt, Ethiopia, Armenia, and Syria.

Even though these debates, and the very subtle arguments that were employed in them, may seem to us idle speculation, it is important to acknowledge that in them Christians were trying to express their own experience of faith and to join it with the witness of the New Testament. Throughout those debates, the church sought to continue affirming the central points of the New Testament witness that have been mentioned above, and which are crucial for Christian faith.

2. THE WORK OF JESUS

Although the question of the person of Christ has occupied the center of attention in christological debate, in truth the work of Christ is at least as important a subject as is his person. Indeed, if we are interested in the person of Christ it is because we call him our Savior. As Melanchthon, Luther's colleague and successor, would say, "to know the benefits of Christ is to know him"—and, in consequence, the opposite is also true, that not knowing the benefits of Christ, not having him as Savior, is not to know him, no matter how much we know about his person and the various theories about it.

From the very beginnings of Christianity, believers have declared that Jesus is Lord and Savior, and have employed various images and metaphors in order to explain and to understand this. Such images are what theologians usually call "theories of atonement," that is, ways of understanding the saving work of Christ. Let us see some of them.

(a) Jesus, payment for sin

This is the best known of all the theories or images of the work of Christ that we shall study here, even though it is neither the only nor probably the most ancient one. According to this view, Jesus came to pay for our sins, and his death at the cross is that payment. For obvious reasons, this is sometimes called the "juridical," "substitutionary," or "satisfaction" theory of atonement. Sometimes, in order to contrast it with the second theory to be expounded here, it is called "objective," and the other one is called "subjective." Although earlier authors described the work of Christ in juridical terms or as payment for sins, the classic formulation of this view comes from Anselm of Canterbury, in the twelfth century.

Anselm proposed his theory of atonement in a famous book called *Why Did God Become Human?* According to Anselm, sin is an injury against God's honor, and therefore whoever sins is in debt to God. In the feudal society in which Anselm lived, when someone's honor was injured, it was thought that it was necessary to repair the damage by honoring that person in ways that would counterbalance the injury itself. In such cases, the importance of the injury depended on the dignity of the offended party, whereas the value of the honor rendered depended on the dignity of the one offering it. Thus, an apparently minor injury to the honor of a monarch was a grave fault; but if a person of low standing wished to honor that same monarch, this would be very difficult, for the value of this person's act would be measured in terms of his or her social position, and not that of the king. If then sin is understood as a debt that sinful humanity has contracted by injuring the honor of the infinite God, such debt can never be paid, for the injury is infinite, and the sinner is not.

It is on this basis that Anselm explains why God became human. Sin, as a human debt, had to be paid by a human being. As a debt against the infinite God, it required an infinite payment. Therefore, the only means to reach an adequate payment for the existing debt was for it to be paid by God made human, so that the payment or "satisfaction" for the debt would be both human and infinite.

This understanding of the work of Christ, which is the most commonly held among Protestants as well as among Catholics, has some advantages and some disadvantages. On the plus side, it certainly communicates the enormity of our sin, which is such that God has to suffer for it. Sin produces pain in God, and is not something that we can dispose of by simply asking for forgiveness, or that can be undone with good intentions or even good actions. Furthermore, God's love is such as to take upon Godself the dire consequences of sin—death and suffering.

On the negative side, this understanding of the work of Christ depicts a wrathful and vindictive God, whose sense of honor is such that every offense has to be paid to the very last drop of blood. In some cases, this even leads some believers to conceive of God the Father as austere and demanding, and God the Son, who gives himself at the cross, as loving and forgiving. Needless to say, this has dire consequences for Christian faith.

Also, this view of the work of Christ is so centered on the cross that the rest of the life of Jesus loses significance. Thus, the Incarnation is only the means whereby God becomes able to pay the price for sin. The Resurrection is simply the vindication, the seal of approval that God pronounces over Jesus. Even though it confirms the value of what took place on the cross, it is not part of the saving work of Christ.

A variation on this view of the work of Christ as payment for sin affirms that Jesus did buy us in the cross, but not from a debt toward God, but rather from the power of Satan. According to this view—which is found already in some of the earliest Christian writers—as a result of sin humankind became enslaved to Satan, who was not ready to grant its freedom except at a very high price. Such was the price paid by Jesus on the cross. The advantage of this old understanding is that it is not God, but Satan, who demands the sacrifice of Jesus, and therefore there is no tendency to establish a contrast between the Father and the Son regarding their love for humanity.

At some points in Christian tradition, especially during the Middle Ages, the understanding of God as wrathful and even vindictive was extended, not only to the Father, but also to the Son. It was at that point that the intercession of the Virgin Mary became crucial as a loving person who is able to understand the human condition.

(b) Jesus, saving example

Another way of interpreting the saving work of Christ, which some have proposed as an alternative to the "juridical" theory, is to see him as a grand example who by his love and his signs of mercy opens the way to God. Although probably not as ancient as some of the other views discussed here, this understanding of the work of Christ gained wide acceptance during the nineteenth and twentieth centuries. According to this view, Christ saves us because, seeing him suffer for us, and seeing in him a love so great that it even forgives those who crucify him, we are invited and moved to love God. Then, moved by that love, we abandon sin and lead a just and holy life.

Sometimes, in order to contrast it with the juridical interpretation, this view is called "subjective," whereas the view of Anselm and others is called "objective." The first to propose it systematically was Abelard, who lived during the twelfth century, as did Anselm of Canterbury. Later, beginning in the nineteenth century, it was the typical way in which liberal theology understood the work of Christ—especially German theologian Albrecht Ritschl, who wrote a vast work in which he refuted the "objective" theory and proposed the alternative of Christ as a saving example.

This theory has the advantage that it does not present God as a petty ruler whose honor has been wounded and who now demands to be paid in blood and suffering. On the contrary, here the alienation between God and humankind is not so much on the side of God as on ours. It is we who, by our sin, and perhaps because we fear God unduly, become increasingly alienated from God. Also, this doctrine points to the affective dimension of sin and of our relationship with God: whereas the juridical interpretation thinks only in terms of debt and payment, this other interpretation speaks in terms of love and of being attracted again to the love of God.

However, this view also has its serious drawbacks. One of them is that it does not seem to take into account the true power and nature of sin. As has already been stated, sin is not just a series of actions that are evil or that oppose the will of God. Sin is an entire state, a way of being, and even a slavery. In order to be freed from sin it does not suffice to wish to be free. Nor does it suffice for someone to give us an example of love and thus to inspire us to act properly.

Another weakness in this theory is that, if the work of Christ is merely a good example, there is no reason we cannot find similar salvation in any other good example—as that of a saintly person or a martyr. Although according to the early proponents of this theory what moves us is that it is God who thus suffers, in its more recent versions it would seem that there is no reason for the incarnation of God in Jesus Christ.

Finally, as in the previous case, this understanding of the work of Christ is so centered on the cross that it is difficult to see the role of the Resurrection. Besides the cross, this theory can see some value in the rest of the life and teachings of Jesus, as indications of the path we are to follow. But it is difficult to see the significance of the Resurrection for our salvation, beyond merely proving that this Jesus whose sufferings inspire us is truly God.

(c) Jesus, conqueror

This interpretation of the work of Christ, often combined with the next we shall study, is the one most frequently found in ancient Christian writers; but it is also a view that has been forgotten or at least ignored in much of the Western theological tradition.

It was only in the twentieth century, thanks to the historical study that Swedish theologian Gustaf Aulén published under the title of *Christus Victor*—Christ the Conqueror—that this third way of understanding the work of Christ was acknowledged in its full significance. Aulén correctly argues that this theory is just as "objective" as the juridical one. It is frequently joined to the fourth theory that will be studied here, since it is thus that it appears in ancient Christian theology—especially in the work of Irenaeus of Lyon, a theologian from the second century. The only reason for separating these two is to clarify their various emphases.

In this understanding of the work of Christ, what the Savior did on our behalf was defeat Satan, who otherwise had us enslaved. In original sin, and in all the rest of its sin, humankind has made itself a servant of Satan, who does not allow it to act as God wishes nor to be what God desires. It is in response to that situation that God becomes incarnate in Jesus Christ and as a human faces all the power of Satan, whom he defeats. As conqueror of Satan, Jesus frees us from sin and from its slavery.

As in the juridical theory, this understanding has the value that it takes the power and scope of sin seriously. However, it does not see the human predicament in terms of a debt requiring payment, but rather in terms of a slavery requiring liberation and victory over the oppressor. Sin is not something of which we can be rid by our own means or efforts—as would seem to be implied in the "subjective" theory—but something of such magnitude that it requires divine intervention.

The other positive point in this view is that it makes the entire life of Jesus significant for our salvation, from his incarnation to his return in glory. The Incarnation is the moment in which God in Jesus enters this humanity, which was subject to Satan. Here among us, through each step in his life and each of his actions, Jesus defeats Satan. This may be seen in the story of the temptations, as well as in the many miracles of Jesus, which are like skirmishes against the powers of evil. But it is seen above all in the three days between the cross and the Resurrection. In the Crucifixion, Satan unleashed all his forces, and for a moment he even seemed to have won. But in rising again Jesus conquered the power of the devil, which from that point on has been broken. This now allows us to have new life, even as we await the day of the final victory with the return of Jesus.

It was within the context of this theory that the ancient church interpreted the descent of Jesus to hell during the time between his death and resurrection. Ephesians says that Jesus "descended into the lower parts of the earth," and that for that reason "when he ascended on high he made captivity itself a captive" (Eph. 4:8-9). Thus, what is understood by the descent into hell in this context is that the Crucifixion was the means whereby Jesus entered the very center of the power of the devil, from whence he returned victorious in his resurrection. Perhaps one could employ here a modern metaphor, and say that Satan believed that he had Jesus in his power, and took him to his headquarters, where he placed him in the safest possible place—"the lower parts," as Ephesians says. But on the third day Jesus turned out to be like a time bomb that exploded powerfully and rose from the dead, by which action not only was he raised, but also the power of Satan to keep humanity in subjection was broken.

The main shortcoming of this view of the work of Christ is that it may be very difficult to envision by us modern people, who are used to thinking in terms of a world in which there are no more realities than those that we see, and who imagine that the only power that evil has is what we freely decide to give it.

(d) Jesus, head of a new humanity

This fourth way of understanding the work of Christ sees him as the founder of a new humanity, of a new body whose head he is. It is grounded on the vision of the New Testament, according to which Adam is the head of a fallen humanity, and Jesus is the head of a restored humanity. Paul declares that "as all die in Adam, so all will be made alive in Christ" (1 Cor. 15:22). According to this view, Jesus is our Savior by inviting us to be joined to him and to his body—the church—just as members form part of a body or branches form part of a vine. As the head of a new humanity, Jesus is the beginning of a new creation. Those who are joined to him share in that new creation and its promise. Furthermore, this new body has a strength that the old did not have, for while Adam "became a living being," Jesus is "a life-giving spirit" (1 Cor. 15:45)—that is to say, that the former has to receive life, whereas the latter bestows life.

As already stated, in the ancient church this understanding of the work of Christ is usually entwined with the view that sees Christ as conqueror of Satan and sin. The manner in which the victory of Christ becomes effective for us is precisely in that he has begun a new humanity, and that when we join him and that new humanity we become partakers of his victory and of his power over sin and over Satan.

This may be seen in the writings of Irenaeus of Lyon, who uses the term *recapitulatio* to refer to the work of Christ. Sometimes it is difficult for us to understand this, because for us today a "recapitulation" is a summary, a brief repetition of what has already been said or written. But etymologically, *recapitulatio* means "reheading"—in Latin, *caput* is "head." This is a word that appears already in the New Testament, particularly in Ephesians 1:10, where we are told that the mystery of God's purpose is "to gather up all things in him." (The Greek word employed here for this gathering is *anakephalaiosis*, which also includes the root *kephale*, "head.") Therefore, when Irenaeus says that Jesus "recapitulated" humankind, what he is saying is that Jesus gave it a new head.

When, as in the case of Irenaeus, the two visions of Jesus as conqueror and as head are combined, this implies that the victory that the Head has achieved will also be—and in a way already is—the victory of the body itself.

When one speaks of Jesus as conqueror, as in the previous image, or as head, as is the case in this one, this involves the entire life of Jesus. It is precisely by becoming human that Jesus is able to head a new humanity. Throughout his entire life, but especially in his death and resurrection, Jesus undoes what was done by Adam.

An added value in this view is that it underscores the solidarity of the human race, both in sin and in salvation. Whereas the old humanity is a body of sin and damnation whose head is Adam, the new humanity is a body of holiness and salvation whose head is Jesus.

The main difficulty in this view of redemption has to do with our modern individualism, which makes it difficult for us to envision how a vast number of individuals can be a single body with one head, or how the resurrection and victory of that head may be the beginning of the resurrection and victory of the entire body.

In summary, the redemptive work of Jesus has been interpreted in various ways—of which the four most common have been outlined. None of them by itself manages to describe all that we owe to Jesus Christ, or all that he does for us. Each of them stresses an important element, and therefore is of value.

It is important to point out that these theories do not exist in isolation from the rest of Christian theology, but are indeed connected with every other aspect of Christian doctrine. This may be seen clearly in the case of the sacraments (which will be studied in another chapter). In general, those who hold to the juridical theory of redemption see baptism as a washing away of sins, or perhaps even as a remission of the debt that had been incurred because of those sins. From the same perspective, Communion becomes another way of attaining such forgiveness, be it through merits (as when it is held that communion is the repeated sacrifice of Jesus) or through repentance (as in much of the more recent Protestant tradition). When one follows the "subjective" view of redemption, one tends to see in the sacraments symbols or reminders that lead us again to see and to acknowledge what Jesus has done for us, and to respond in love and repentance. When one sees Jesus as conqueror of the powers of evil, and especially when he is seen also as the head of a new humanity, baptism becomes the act of being grafted into the body of that new humanity, and communion—as well as worship in general—becomes the means by which we are nourished by that body and remain united to it.

3. DIMENSIONS OF SALVATION

(a) Salvation and the Savior's work

Throughout the centuries, Christians have called Jesus "our Savior," that is, the one who brings salvation to us. However, not always have we been completely clear as to what it is that we mean by "salvation." Also in this case, as in the matter of Christ's saving work, there are different emphases or perspectives that must be clarified.

1. Most commonly we think of salvation as the forgiveness of sins, so that we may enter into heaven. Normally, this understanding of salvation goes hand in hand with one of the first two views of redemption just studied, either the "juridical" or the "subjective." Those who believe that the work of Christ consists in paying for our sins (the juridical theory) see salvation as the fact that, thanks to that payment by Jesus, the way is now open for us to enter into eternal life. Those who see the work of Christ mostly in "subjective" terms, that is, who see Jesus as inspiring us to serve and to follow God, also tend to think that this allows us to love God in such a way that we may enter heaven. In both cases, salvation consists in admission to eternal life.

It is important to point out that such an understanding of salvation is very close to that of the Gnostics, who believed that salvation consisted in acquiring the secrets that would allow their souls to flee from this bodily prison and ascend to the spiritual heights. Christianity has traditionally rejected such doctrines, not only because they claim that salvation is attained by means of a secret knowledge, but also because they affirm that salvation consists in escaping from this world, which after all is God's creation. When one reflects on these matters, it is clear that, although Christianity has rejected Gnosticism repeatedly, the temptation of Gnostic interpretations of life and of reality is always present.

2. Those who see the saving work of Christ in terms of the last two theories discussed above tend to see salvation in a different way. Certainly salvation does bring eternal life, but it is much more than that. Salvation consists in being joined to Christ, the Conquering Head of a new humanity. We enter into life eternal, not because we have a pass or a ticket, but rather because we are united to the Lord of life, who in his resurrection conquered death itself— or, as the ancients would say, "killed death."

This means that salvation, besides being the promise of eternal life, is also the process whereby God frees us from the power of sin. Every act or moment in life in which we see signs of that liberation is also a saving act of God. This is true, not only of the strictly religious and the personal, but also of the social, cultural, political, and economic dimensions of life.

Very often in the Old Testament the word "salvation" appears in the context of a deliverance. For instance, when David is delivered from the hand of Saul, he sings to God as "the horn of my salvation" (2 Sam. 22:3). Sometimes in the Revised Standard Version the same word is translated as "deliverance" (Exod. 14:13) or as "victory" (Judg. 15:18). All of these actions of God, which are as an image and a promise of the great saving action in Jesus Christ, are also acts of salvation.

3. In any case, it is important to remember that our salvation is not only our concern, but also God's. It is not a matter of our having to find a way to be saved. It is also and above all a matter of God, our Creator, having an interest in saving us for the purposes for which we were created. Perhaps we should imagine an artist— a sculptor—whose work has somehow been damaged, and the artist now tries to "save." God, as supreme artist of the universe, seeks to save creation.

This is a very important point, because too often there are Christians who speak of salvation as if it were something that we have to wrest from God, as if God were seeking a way to condemn us, and we had to find a way to frustrate such an intent. (Sometimes this is related to what has been said above, that the juridical or "objective" theory of redemption leads us to think in terms of God the Father as wrathful and vindictive, and the Son as loving and forgiving.) In the matter of salvation, God is not our enemy, but our ally.

(b) An integral salvation

Whereas in the last chapter we spoke of the scope of creation and also of sin, it is now time to emphasize the vast scope of salvation. As has been repeatedly stated before, from the very beginnings of the life of the church there were those who divided reality into two, attributing to God the origin and the rule of only one part of that reality. Thus, Gnostics affirmed that the spiritual world is the work of God, but not the material world. Likewise, they claimed that the human spirit is divine, and that the body has nothing to do with the final destiny of the spirit.

On the basis of such opinions, Gnostics as well as others of similar tendencies would limit salvation to the spirit, which returns to the spiritual realm, and declare that the body cannot be saved. Although these and similar doctrines have existed and even exist to this day among Christians who believe themselves to be perfectly orthodox, the truth is that from a very early date the church at large, basing its decision on the witness of Scripture, rejected such opinions, which among other things led to confusion regarding the nature of a holy life.

Such doctrines produce confusion regarding the nature of a holy life because if the body has nothing to do with salvation, the two obvious alternatives are quite dangerous.

The first, which is also the most common, is to come to the conclusion that, since the body does not share in salvation, and may even be an obstacle to it, it must be repressed and punished. On such grounds there have been many who have tortured themselves or who have carried fasting to the point of affecting their health. Furthermore, since the body has nothing to do with eternal matters, there is no reason to be worried about the bodies of other people that may be broken and even destroyed in order to attain their salvation. That was the reasoning behind many of the practices of the Inquisition. In less extreme cases, there are Christians who debate whether the hungry should be fed and the ill should be healed even though there is little chance that they will be converted, on the basis that what we must seek is the salvation of their souls, and that the only reason to feed or heal them is to invite them to be converted.

The second consequence is its opposite. If the body has nothing to do with salvation, why not simply let it follow its own inclinations? Strange as it may seem, there were Gnostics who followed this doctrine to the point of becoming libertines. And there are Christians who, perhaps without going to such extremes, rationalize their actions in a similar fashion.

If human beings are wholly God's creatures, and God loves the entire human being, salvation must include the whole person, body as well as soul. This is why the Apostles' Creed affirms our belief in "the resurrection of the body"—or, as the Greek original says, "of the flesh."

The holistic nature of salvation can be seen in the very word employed for it in the New Testament: *soteria*. This word means both salvation in the sense of returning to God, and healing; it is the translators who in each case have to decide whether to translate it as "salvation" or "healing." A typical case is the often quoted verse in Acts 4:12: "There is salvation in no one else, for there is no other name under heaven given among mortals by which we must be saved." What is being discussed in the context is the healing of a man who is lame, and therefore the verse could be translated as: "There is healing in no one else, for there is no other name . . . by which we must be healed." In truth, the best course would be a translation that would include both elements, for that is precisely what is meant by the word employed there. Every healing act is also a saving act, and vice versa.

But there is more. If salvation is God's action so that the divine purposes for creation are fulfilled, it cannot be limited to human beings. In its fullest sense, salvation culminates in the restoration of all creation—heaven as well as earth. To this we shall return in the last chapter.

(c) The process of salvation: justification and sanctification

In a sense, God's saving action begins at the very moment of the Fall. As soon as the human creature sins and the entirety of creation is corrupted, God begins to act in order to undo sin and its consequences. This is why repeatedly the Old Testament employs words such as "salvation" and "savior" for events and individuals that might seem to be far removed from the salvation brought about by Christ the Savior, but which are a sign that the God of salvation is constantly acting in history.

From another perspective, salvation for each of us begins with "justification." Justification is the divine action that restores our relationship with the God of all justice. Without being just, we cannot face the just God.

How is justification attained? This was one of the main points of debate during the Protestant Reformation in the sixteenth century. Although the matter is much more complex, one may say that the main point at issue between Catholics and Protestants was that Catholics held that a person had to be just and do works of justice so that God would count that person just, whereas Protestants insisted that God declares us just by the infinite divine mercy, and that therefore all that is necessary for salvation is that faith that allows us to accept the divine decree of justification.

The classical formulation of this Protestant doctrine is often called "imputed justice," which means that God declares us just, not because God sees justice or righteousness in us, but rather because God assigns or imputes to us the

94

justice and righteousness of Jesus Christ. Hence Luther's famous phrase, that a believer is *simul justus et peccator*—at the same time just and a sinner. What justifies us is not the absence of sin, but the grace of God who declares us just.

This emphasis on unmerited justification can easily lead us to forget another important aspect of salvation—sanctification. Thus we frequently hear in Protestant churches that all that we have to do in order to be saved is to believe in Jesus Christ. This is then understood to mean that it suffices to accept Jesus, and we are saved—which would be true if salvation consisted only in justification. But this is not entirely true if salvation includes the entire process whereby we come to be what God wishes us to be—that is to say, if sanctification is part of salvation.

God accepts us even while we are still sinners, and freely declares us justified. But what God wishes for us—full salvation—is that we be truly just, that we be as God intends, that is, that through the work of the Holy Spirit in ourselves we be sanctified.

Among Protestants, generally the Reformed tradition—that is to say, that which stems from John Calvin—has underscored sanctification more than the Lutheran tradition. Within the Reformed tradition, John Wesley has become known for his emphasis on "progress toward perfection." According to Wesley, the task of every believer is to move toward perfection with the help of the Holy Spirit.

This led to a debate between Wesley and several theologians of his time, about whether such perfection is attainable in this life. Although declaring that he himself lacked much to attain such perfection, Wesley insisted that it is indeed attainable as a special gift of God, and that it is necessary to preach about it because otherwise believers will forsake the path of sanctification. It is from this aspect of Wesleyan tradition that the "holiness churches" stem.

Finally, no matter how much we move ahead in the process of sanctification, salvation does not reach its fullness until the final consummation of all things. It is then, in the midst of a renewed creation that serves the will of God—a new heaven and a new earth—that we will truly be what God intends us to be—that we shall finally find our true being. As Paul says, our life is hidden with Christ in God, and when Christ is revealed at the consummation of all times, then we too will be revealed (Col. 3:3-4).

V. WHAT IS THE CHURCH?

All through the centuries, believers in Christ have lived in "churches." The church, we say, is the community of believers. And yet, if the spirit of division and dissension among Christians is manifest anywhere, it is in the church. Some churches claim to be the only true one, and reject the others as false or at least deficient. Others say that the doctrine of the church is not important, for the church is no more than a group of Christians who gather in order to support one another in the faith; but then they insist that all their members must agree in every detail of doctrine, as if they were the final judge in matters of faith. Some believers change churches as they change a shirt or a dress, perhaps because they did not like something that someone said, because they disagree with a decision taken, because they do not like the music, because the worship service seems too "cold," or too "noisy," or for some other reason.

All of this points to the need for theology to clarify what the church is. If, as was suggested in the first chapter, one of the main functions of theology is to critique the life and proclamation *of the church* in the light of the gospel, it is clear that one of the fundamental questions for theology is precisely the doctrine of the church—what in technical terms is called "ecclesiology." In this chapter we shall see repeatedly that ecclesiology must take into account, not only the doctrine of the church in theoretical or ideal terms, but also its social and historical reality. Certainly, the power of the Holy Spirit is made manifest in the church, but so is the power of social, economic, political, and cultural circumstances. It is possible to study the church in terms of its spiritual reality, ignoring its social reality; it is also possible to study it in social terms, making use of sociological instruments, and ignoring the presence of the Spirit in the church. But neither the one nor the other by itself will give us an adequate view of the church.

Ecclesiology developed slowly in the early church, as circumstances made it necessary. For the early Christians, the church was above all an experience, the context within which they lived and they experienced their faith. It was with the passing of years, as divisions appeared and with them also arose debates as to whether the true church was this group or that, that arguments and treatises were produced about the nature of the church, and about how to distinguish the true church from the false.

The first such discussions revolved around the challenge of Gnosticism and its claim to possess a secret doctrine communicated by Jesus in private to one of his apostles, who in turn transmitted it to Gnostic teachers. Over against such claims of a secret and private succession, the orthodox writers of the second and third centuries proposed an open and public succession. According to them, in certain churches—such as those of Rome, Ephesus, and Antioch—there were bishops who could point to a direct succession from the apostles who had been in those cities to themselves. Since all these bishops agreed on the essential tenets of the Christian message, and rejected Gnostic teachings, the true church, the one that supports correct doctrine, is that which agrees and is in communion with those bishops, and not any group founded by a teacher claiming secret knowledge.

It is important to note that in its early stages the principle of apostolic succession did not deny the validity of the ministry of those who could not declare themselves to be direct successors of the apostles, as long as their doctrine agreed with that of those who could claim such succession. Therefore, although the bishop of Carthage was not a direct successor of the apostles, his doctrine and ministry were confirmed in that he agreed with the witness of the apostolic churches. It was only later that some churches turned the "apostolic succession" into an almost mechanical matter, so that for an ordination to be valid it must claim an uninterrupted line of ordinations going back to the apostles.

In the third century, in North Africa, Cyprian of Carthage wrote an important treatise *On the Unity of the Church*. It was Cyprian who coined the famous phrases: "outside the church there is no salvation," and "one who does not have the church as a mother cannot have God as a father." Cyprian was concerned over a schismatic group that had abandoned the church because it did not consider it sufficiently pure—because it had forgiven those who had lapsed in times of persecution and later wished to return to the church. It was against these schismatics that Cyprian penned his two famous phrases.

Something similar happened in the times of Augustine, toward the end of the fourth century, when another group—this time the Donatists—left the rest of the church for similar reasons as those used by the earlier schismatics in times of Cyprian. But already by the time of Augustine the church counted on the support of the state, and therefore the matter of determining who was the true church had enormous political and even economic importance, for only that true church could count on government support. Augustine himself wrote several treatises against the Donatists, where the essential argument was that the true church is the one that exists throughout the earth, and is in communion with the churches whose bishops can point to an uninterrupted succession beginning with the apostles.

From that point on, ecclesiology continued developing, most often as a means to refute various schismatic groups—that is, to argue that the true church is this one, and not that other particular group. It is partly for that reason that some Protestants have paid little attention to ecclesiology, and that those who have written on the doctrine of the church have usually been more concerned about refuting the claims of the Roman Church, and claiming that theirs is indeed a true church.

1. IMAGES OF THE CHURCH IN THE NEW TESTAMENT

Although the church is a central theme in a great deal of the New Testament, it is never defined. What the New Testament offers is rather a series of images or metaphors that allow us to understand a particular element or aspect of the church. These images are many, to the point that some claim to have found more than a hundred of them. However, there are a few that already seem to be central in the New Testament itself, and which have also influenced the manner in which the church has understood itself through the centuries. Let us look at some of them.

(a) The church as the Body of Christ

This image, which appears repeatedly in the Pauline Epistles, is the most common in the New Testament. (It is so common, that the word itself, "member," which we employ today for anyone who belongs to the church, actually comes from that image, for it refers to being a "member" of this "body" that is the church.) Sometimes, as in Ephesians and Colossians, this image is used explicitly as a way of understanding the church. At other times, such as in Romans 12 and 1 Corinthians 12, it is used in order to draw from it consequences regarding the manner in which the members of the church are to relate among themselves.

In Ephesians and Colossians, the image of the "body" is closely united to that of the "head": God "has made him the head over all things for the church, which is his body" (Eph. 1:22-23); "He is the head of the body, the church" (Col. 1:18); "Christ is the head of the church, the body of which he is the Savior" (Eph. 5:23); "The head, from whom the whole body . . ." (Col. 2:19).

This shows that one of the main emphases of this image is the close relationship, both of unity and of subjection, between Christ and the church. Christ is not only the founder of the church, as one who founds a philosophical school or a social club. Christ is the *head* of the church, and as its head he is constantly manifested in the life of the body, so that without him the body has no life.

Second, this image of the church as the Body of Christ is employed in the New Testament in order to underline the close relationship that must exist among Christians, even though they may have different gifts or functions. This theme appears both in Romans and in 1 Corinthians. In the passage in Romans 12:4-8 where Paul discusses the diversity of gifts, the key phrase is "so we, who are many, are one body in Christ, and individually we are members one of another" (Rom. 12:5).

Note that here Paul says not only that Christians are members of the Body of Christ, but also that they are members each of the others. The interdependency of the various members of a body is not limited to their common relationship with the head, but is also direct. Each member depends on all the rest.

Also in 1 Corinthians 12, Paul deals with the image of the church as a Body of Christ, once again in order to underline unity in the midst of the diversity of gifts: "For just as the body is one and has many members, and all the members of the body, though many, are one body, so it is with Christ" (1 Cor. 12:12). "Indeed, the body does not consist of one member but of many" (1 Cor. 12:14). As in

Romans, the image of the church as the Body of Christ shows that diversity, far from causing division or strife, is an essential aspect of the unity of the Body of Christ. Diversity is not opposed to unity, but rather produces it, just as the diversity of members gives unity to the body.

However, in this passage Paul uses the image of the church as the Body of Christ in order to point to a third characteristic of that body, beyond its unity with Christ and its inner unity: this is a body in which those who would seem to be of lesser value are most important:

> On the contrary, the members of the body that seem to be weaker are indispensable, and those members of the body that we think less honorable we clothe with greater honor, and our less respectable members are treated with greater respect; whereas our more respectable members do not need this. But God has so arranged the body, giving the greater honor to the inferior member, that there may be no dissension within the body, but the members may have the same care for one another. (1 Cor. 12:22-25)

One of the central themes of this entire epistle, especially of the chapters that lead to chapter 13, is the scandal that takes place when believers gather in order to celebrate Communion, and some bring enough food to be filled and even to become drunk, while others hardly have enough to eat. Here Paul warns them that, if they are truly the Body of Christ, they must be a body in which special attention is given to the poor and humble that some seem to regard with contempt. It is precisely because the church is the *Body* of Christ, that shortly before the text quoted above Paul warns his readers that any who eat and drink unworthily, not paying attention to such marginalized people, "without discerning the body," that is, without realizing that this body is different, "eat and drink judgment against themselves" (1 Cor. 11:29).

Thus, as body of that head, which is Christ, the church (1) is joined and subject to Christ; (2) is one within itself; and (3) must show particular respect for those who are usually least respected.

In all of this, it is interesting to note that the New Testament does not seem to stress what today most people understand when they hear that the church is the Body of Christ, that is, that the church is the instrument by which Christ acts today in the world—as when we say that we are the feet and the hands of Jesus. This use of the image of the church as the Body of Christ, which is not that of the New Testament, is a reflection of our modern pragmatism, for which the "body" is simply an instrument of the will. In the New Testament, it is not a matter of the church being the Body of Christ because it does his will, but rather of doing his will because it is his body.

In the ancient church the image of the church as the Body of Christ was understood as an affirmation of its role in salvation. Thus, in Romans 5–8 Paul contrasts two sorts of humanity, which are defined by their two heads: Adam and Christ. This is the background of his famous statement (1 Cor. 15:22): "For as all die in Adam, so all will be made alive in Christ." On this basis, Irenaeus understood that the resurrection of Christ, head of the body, is the beginning of the resurrection of the church—which implies that in order to partake of the benefits of the resurrection of Christ one has to be joined to him as a member of his body, the church. It is in this sense that Cyprian, a century later, declared that "outside the church there is no salvation." Although in some cases this principle has been abused in order to threaten with eternal damnation those who do not agree with the doctrines and government of a particular church, the truth is that, if the church is indeed the Body of Christ, it is difficult to see how one can claim to be "in Christ" without being part of that body.

(b) The church as people of God

Another image that appears frequently in the New Testament, in the ancient church, and through the centuries, is that of the church as "people of God." This image is found in Romans, where Paul discusses the relationship between Jews and those Gentiles who have accepted Christ, and in order to refer to the latter, he quotes Hosea: "Those who were not my people I will call 'my people'" (Rom. 9:25). The same idea is found in the oft quoted words of 1 Peter 2:9-10: "But you are a chosen race, a royal priesthood, a holy nation, God's own people. . . . Once you were not a people, but now you are God's people."

One of the main values of this image is that it underlines the continuity between the Old and the New Testaments. In both cases, the theme is the relationship between God and God's people—Israel in the Old Testament, and the church in the New. This is particularly clear in the quote from 1 Peter, where other characteristics formerly attributed exclusively to Israel are now applied also to the church: chosen race, royal priesthood, holy nation. It is precisely because of this continuity between the people of God in both testaments that the church can see in the Old Testament the Word of God for itself.

This image also counteracts other more hierarchical or structural views of the church. This has been particularly important for Roman Catholicism, which at one time tended to confuse the church with its hierarchy, and where therefore the new theology that has become dominant after the Second Vatican Council prefers to speak of the church as God's people. This in turn has led to a greater democratization, and more emphasis on lay ministries.

Finally, the image of the church as God's people reminds us that this is a *pilgrim* people. This theme, central to the earlier books of the Old Testament, is also central in the last books of the New, where the church is spoken of as a pilgrim people (1 Pet. 2:11), and where both Israel and the church are marching toward a better homeland (Heb. 11:14-16).

This image risks letting us think that, now that the church is the people of God, the ancient people of Israel have been rejected. Paul firmly rejects and extensively refutes such a notion (Rom. 9–15). But in spite of this, through the centuries there have been Christians who have committed atrocities against Jews, arguing that now that the church is the new Israel, the old Israel is cursed. This is a tragic error of which Christians must always beware!

(c) Other images of the church

As stated above, the New Testament employs many images to refer to the church. The image of "bride of Christ" (based on Ephesians 5:23-27, and above all on Revelation 19:7; 21:2, 9; 22:17) has been much used, partly because it seems to refer to the mystical union between Christ and the church, and partly also because it has been used for insisting that, just as Christ is the Lord of the church, so is the husband the lord of his wife. As employed in Revelation, it has more the sense of "betrothed": the church is anxiously expecting its final union with its husband. Perhaps this is the element that should be underlined in this image: the church awaits the consummation of its union with Christ.

One of the reasons the image of Christ as husband of the church has been so popular, especially in the Western church, is that it has been used as a means of expressing the mystical union. In the Eastern churches it has been more common to speak of a direct union with God, so that sometimes it would seem that the individual is lost in the ocean of divinity. As an alternative to this sort of mysticism, traditionally Western mysticism has referred to its experiences of union with Christ in terms such as the wedding of the soul with its Lord. The problem with this use of the image is its excessively individualistic tone, for now the "bride of Christ" is no longer the church as a whole, but the individual soul.

Several of the many images employed in the New Testament to speak of the church point to its communal character, its intimate relationship with God, and the bond that must exist among its members. Thus, the church as the household of God (Eph. 2:19) reminds us of its intimate union with God and among its members. The church as a building (1 Pet. 2:4-5) is a similar image to that of the church as body, except that in this case, instead of speaking of believers as "members," they are "stones." Also, this image underscores the dynamic nature of the church, which is not to remain the same, but must be built up. The church as a flock (John 10:16, Acts 20:28-29) and its Lord as a shepherd (Matt. 9:36; 26:31; John 10:16; Heb. 13:30; 1 Pet. 2:25) is a similar image to that of the church as a people; but it underscores the nature of the church as pilgrim, seeking better pastures, and in need of the guidance and defense of its shepherd.

(d) Social realities of the church in the New Testament

If in the New Testament we had only the images of the church just mentioned, one could imagine that the church at the times of the apostles was ideal. However, that is not the case. In the very church of Jerusalem, where we are told that there was a profound love, and that believers shared all things, the episode occurs of Ananias and Sapphira (Acts 5:1-11). In Corinth there were divisions, gossip, doubt, and immorality. The Epistle to the Galatians shows that the relationship between Paul and Peter was sometimes tense. The book of Revelation mentions several faults in the churches to which it addresses individual letters. Therefore, the church in the New Testament is neither ideal nor perfect.

It is precisely about such a church, with all its imperfections, that we are told that it is the Body of Christ, people of God, bride to the Lamb. These contrasting realities imply that an ecclesiology that is faithful to the truth of the church must affirm at the same time that it is Body of Christ, and bride to the Lamb, but that it also is a community of sinners, affected by all the afflictions and para-doxes of the human condition.

2. THE MARKS OF THE CHURCH

The Nicene Creed, used by the Roman Catholic Church as well as by Eastern Orthodoxy and by most Protestant churches, affirms that we believe in "one holy catholic and apostolic church." Traditionally these have been said to be the four marks or signs of the true church of Jesus Christ: one, holy, catholic, apostolic. Let us look at them in that order.

(a) The church is one

The above-mentioned images imply that the church is one. Indeed, it would be difficult to say that there are several bodies of Christ, and even more difficult to affirm that Christ has several brides. This clearly does not mean that the word *church* cannot be used in the plural. Already in the New Testament we find that there are churches in various cities. They are all "churches." But it is also true that they are all part of the "church," in singular. In conse-quence, one of the great problems that ecclesiology has to deal with is the unity of the church. There have been different ways to approach this issue:

1. *Unity in the ancient church* was understood in terms of partici-pating of the same Communion, mutual acknowledgment, and agreement on the essential points of Christian doctrine.

In the ancient church, the most common practice was for each local church—that is, the church in each city—to elect its own pastor or bishop. However, in order to show that this bishop was part of the universal church, in his consecration other bishops participated—usually at least three—com-ing from nearby churches. If for some reason the person elected did not seem worthy of the position, or if his doctrine was doubtful, a "synod" or gathering of the bishops of the area decided on the matter.

Normally in each city there was only one church. In some cases, when in a single city the number of believers was such or they were so widely dis-persed that they could not gather weekly to celebrate Communion, a fragment of the bread used in the Communion service in the main church was taken to the other congregations and placed with the bread to be used for Communion there, as an indication that the church in that city, although gathering in various places, was indeed only one.

What was not allowed was the existence in the same city or area of two or more churches, each separate from the other. When such happened, an appeal was made to the bishops of other churches, who would gather in a synod in order to examine the issues and determine which of the two churches would be in Communion with the rest of the church.

Progressively, the churches were organized by regions in which a metropolitan bishop enjoyed a certain priority over the others. Eventually the bishops of some of the ancient and important churches—Jerusalem, Antioch, Alexandria, Constantinople, and Rome—were called "patriarchs."

In that ancient system, unity was centered in Communion, according to the words of the apostle Paul: "The cup of blessing that we bless, is it not a sharing in the blood of Christ? The bread that we break, is it not a sharing in the body of Christ? Because there is one bread, we who are many are one body, for we all partake of the one bread" (1 Cor. 10:16-17). Therefore, as long as the churches in various places acknowledged one another by participating in the same Communion, so that in their services they would pray for one another, and their members could partake of Communion in one another's gatherings, it was felt that the unity of the church had not been broken.

2. In the Middle Ages, unity came to be seen as subjection to a single hierarchy. This was true especially in western Europe, where the disappearance of the ancient Roman Empire left a vacuum that in many ways the church filled. The result was a centralizing process, so that eventually it was commonly held that the unity of the church consisted in subjection to the pope.

Although the Roman Church tried to impose its authority over the Eastern churches, the latter never accepted such authority. Finally, the schism between the Latin-speaking West and the Greek-speaking East took place in the year 1054, when the pope's representatives broke Communion with the Patriarch of Constantinople and therefore with the rest of the Eastern Church. Although part of what was being debated was the pope's authority, it was still believed that the main sign of the union of the church was mutual acceptance in Communion, and the clear sign of the breach was the mutual exclusion from Communion.

3. With the advent of the Protestant Reformation, the emphasis shifted toward unity in doctrine. Although Rome insisted on hierarchical unity, the reformers declared that the unity of the church should be manifest above all in its doctrinal unity. According to Calvin, wherever the Word of God is properly preached and the sacraments are practiced as Jesus instituted them, there is the true church of Jesus Christ to be found. Although the government of the church is necessary, the unity of the church is not in its government or structure, but in its doctrine and practice.

Calvin and the main reformers agreed that it was not necessary for all the churches to be in total agreement on every point of doctrine. According to them, some points of doctrine are essential, and some are not. Thus, that there is only one God, that Jesus Christ is God's Son, and that he is our Savior, are essential points of doctrine. Exactly what happens to the souls of the dead, whether Communion is to be taken seated, standing, or kneeling, and other similar matters, are of secondary importance. The same is true of the various polities, such as the Congregational, the Presbyterian, or the Episcopal. Therefore, it is possible to acknowledge as a true church, and as part of the one church of Jesus Christ, a group with which we do not agree on such secondary matters. Likewise, Calvin affirms that in the Roman Church, by the mere fact that in it the Word of God is still preached and the sacraments are administered, there is at least a "vestige of a church."

4. In more recent times this situation has become more complicated, for churches have tended to divide over all sorts of doctrinal disagreements. The situation was made even more complicated by migration to the Western Hemisphere and other areas, where each group took its own ecclesiastical traditions. As a result, in places such as the United States and Latin America, it is not unusual to find several churches of various denominations in a single city or village.

Although at the beginning Lutherans and Reformed acknowledged each other as true churches, there soon appeared more extreme elements in both traditions, insisting that certain points of Reformed theology—or of Lutheran theology—were absolutely essential. Later there were divisions between those Reformed who followed strict Calvinism and the Arminians. Meanwhile, the churches of the tradition often called "Anabaptist" continued growing and multiplying, and in England another church developed, which while taking much from the Reformed tradition also retained much of the Catholic. Calvin had established a distinction between essential and secondary doctrines. The problem was simply that what some took to be secondary others considered essential.

In Europe, this gave rise to a number of territorial or national churches, so that Anglicans centered in England, Presbyterians in Scotland, and so on. However, when arriving in the Western Hemisphere and other zones to which they went, immigrants proceeding from those various places brought with them their churches, their doctrines, and their traditions. Scots brought Presbyterianism. Germans and Scandinavians brought Lutheranism. The English brought Anglicanism, Methodism, Congregationalism, and the Baptist tradition.

In the new lands, for various reasons, those churches continued dividing. In the United States, the issues surrounding the Civil War brought about the division of several denominations into a "Northern" and a "Southern" branch.

The result of all of this has been an enormous diversity of denominations. Many of them no longer even ask what is the unity of the church. Others simply affirm that unity is not to be sought beyond agreement in doctrine—that all the churches that agree on the essential points of the gospel are a single "invisible" church of Jesus Christ.

The difficulty lies in that many of those churches, while saying that they are a single church in the essentials of the faith, still compete among themselves. When they do not compete, they ignore one another, so that a member of a local church knows more about members of the same denomination in distant areas than about another church of a different denomination across the street. This is probably the greatest difficulty that Protestant ecclesiology will have to deal with in the twenty-first century.

5. This has given origin to the modern ecumenical movement, which is an attempt to seek and manifest the unity of the church. The modern ecumenical movement began among Protestants, mostly in the "mission field," where the division and competition among churches was a clear impediment to the preaching of the gospel. As a result of ecumenical discussion regarding the unity of the church, most participants in those discussions agree at least on the following points regarding that unity.

In a way, the unity of the church is a given; it is a gift of God. The church is one, not because all its members agree among themselves, or because there are no divisions or strife, but because the church is the Body of Christ. All Christians, no matter whether they know it or not, and no matter whether they will it or not, are joined as members of a single body. If they are not joined in that body, they are not joined with Christ, and they therefore cannot be Christians.

In a different sense, the unity of the church is something that all Christians must seek. If there can only be one Body of Christ, any division or strife within that body is a sign of disease—of disease, not in the head, who is Jesus Christ, but in the members.

Therefore, when we say that we believe in the "one" church, we are saying that we believe that in Christ we are one, and at the same time we are confessing that our divisions are a sign of sin, and an indication that our obedience is still wanting.

As to the nature of the unity we are to seek, there are diverse opinions. At one extreme, there are those who hold that the unity of the church requires a single organization—for example, that all be subject to the pope or to some other common system of government. At the other extreme, there are those who hold that unity of doctrine and mutual acknowledgment suffice. The first position seems to ignore that the church has never been one in that sense, for even at the height of the power of the papacy that power never encompassed the entire church. The second extreme can easily serve as an excuse not to seek concrete means of expressing and living our unity. In such cases, we are content with declaring that we are one, while we continue competing with one another, while each denomination is concerned almost exclusively with its own agenda, and the prayer of Jesus is not fulfilled in us "that they may all be one . . . so that the world may believe that you have sent me" (John 17:21).

(b) The church is holy

On studying the historical development of ecclesiology, as well as what is being written and said today about the church, it is obvious that a constant problem for ecclesiology has been the tension between affirming that the church is (or must be, or ought to be) holy, and the historical and sociological reality of that very church. On repeating the Nicene Creed, millions of Christians affirm that they believe in the "holy church." But those same Christians sin, see others sinning, and know that even their pastors and leaders are sinners like themselves. Throughout history, theologians and believers in general have attempted to resolve this conflict in various ways.

1. First solution: creating a holier church. A manner in which some have attempted to respond to this reality is to abandon a church that seems to them too sinful, in order to create another that will be more faithful to the biblical imagery of what the church is to be. Thus every year dozens of new denominations and independent churches are born out of the desire to leave behind what they consider the sinfulness of the existing churches.

This manner of solving the contrast between the church's calling and its historical reality appeared very early in the history of Christianity. It developed especially as a way of solving the question of what to do with the believers who had committed grievous sins. Already in the second century, Hermas, the author of The *Shepherd,* who was writing in Rome, held that after the initial forgiveness of baptism only one other forgiveness was possible, and that after that all grievous sins could only be erased through the "second baptism" in blood, that is, martyrdom. Soon—it is not known exactly how early—the custom appeared of requiring believers who professed to repent from grievous sins to confess them publicly before the congregation, and for them to be restored to the communion of the church only after a period of penance and excommunication—which could well last up to several years. In the third century, in Rome as well as elsewhere, some began claiming that believers who had committed fornication, homicide, or apostasy could never be forgiven. When Bishop Calixtus, in Rome, allowed some believers who had committed fornication to follow the normal process of public confession and restoration, Hippolytus abandoned the church and created his own. In North Africa, also in the third century, Novatian withdrew from the rest of the church because it was ready to restore those who had fallen into apostasy during persecution. The same issue was posed again in the fourth century, when the Donatists withdrew from the rest of the church for similar reasons.

This option is attractive in that it condemns the sins of those who consider themselves Christians, and calls them to holiness. However, it is deficient for two reasons. The first is the empirical fact that soon the new church, founded on the claim of holiness, is not holy enough for some, who then feel called to abandon it, so that the cycle continues and divisions multiply in perpetuity. The second is that such an attitude denies two of the fundamental characteristics of the church: its unity and its message of love. It is obvious that it denies the unity of the church, for the immediate result is that the church divides. The message of love is denied since the church, instead of being a community calling sinners to repentance, and raising and upholding the fallen, becomes a community of judgment and condemnation.

2. Second solution: creating two levels of the church. Another way of solving the tension between the theological vision of the church and its historical reality is to claim that there are two levels of Christians, and that therefore, even though the church as a whole is not as faithful as it should be, there are always some who are more committed. Although there are vast differences between the two movements, this is both the monastic and the pietist solution.

Medieval monasticism is based on the distinction between the "commandments" of God and the "counsels of perfection." That distinction is based on Matthew 19:21, where Jesus says to the rich young man: "If you wish to be perfect, go, sell your possessions, and give the money to the poor." Commandments must be obeyed by all Christians, and this the young man had done. In contrast, the counsels of perfection are only for those who wish to be perfect. These counsels are mainly poverty (on the basis of this text) and celibacy (on the basis of 1 Corinthians 7:38, where Paul says that it is good to marry, but it is best to remain celibate). The result of these views was a large number of monastic communities that sought to live the Christian life at a higher level than the rest of the population. It was there that a higher holiness could be attained, and it was partly because it included such communities that the church could claim to be holy.

Pietism arose among Protestants in the eighteenth century. Its main founder, Philipp Spener, hoped to reform and revitalize the church by creating in it small groups that would be "schools of piety" or "small churches within the church." These groups would devote themselves to biblical study, to prayer, and to works of charity, thus doing what the rest of believers did not seem to be doing, and recovering the holiness of the church. In England, Methodism followed a similar route.

Such reforming movements, although having a significant impact in the life of the church, do not solve the dilemma of sin within a church that calls itself "holy." Furthermore, eventually they too follow the same process of those churches that withdraw from others in order to be holier: the movement loses its initial impetus, and other new movements break away from it in order to claim greater holiness.

3. Third solution: the holy church is the invisible church. This solution holds a certain attraction. It certainly takes into account that within the whole community of believers there are some more faithful and sincere than the rest. Using biblical terminology, it is said that in the church there is both "wheat and tares" (Matt. 13:24-30), and that distinguishing between the two is God's task, and not ours. This has been the traditional response of those who defend the existing church against the reforming impulses of those who propose one of the two other solutions mentioned. The distinction is then made between a "visible church," in which the actions of the "tares" are evident, and an "invisible church," which only God knows, whose members are holy, and which is therefore holy.

The distinction between the visible and the invisible church goes back at least to the time of Augustine, in the fourth century. It has its value, but also its dangers. Its main asset is that it avoids the excessive sacralization of the institutional church, admitting the possibility that some of its members may not really be part of the invisible church, and that some that apparently are outside the church may belong to it. Its main danger is precisely in the opposite extreme: imagining that the church does not need an institutional reality, or that one can be joined to Christ and his church without belonging to a community of the faithful organized as a social body. Throughout history, the first of these extremes has most frequently appeared in the more traditional churches—especially those that have held a dominant position within their societies—and the other extreme has been more common among reforming elements—especially those that emphasize personal experience and the presence of the Spirit.

4. Another possible solution: redefining holiness. At least part of the problem lies in the way in which we have grown accustomed to thinking about holiness. We say that a "holy" person is one who behaves in a certain way. In this sense, holiness lies in conduct. Therefore, a church where sin still exists cannot be holy. However, holiness does not refer exclusively or even primarily to conduct. In the Bible, places or objects can be "holy"—and this certainly does not refer to their conduct!

What makes something holy is the presence of God—more specifically, of the Spirit of God, who is also called "Holy." Strictly speaking, only One is holy, and that is God. The land on which Moses treads is holy, because God is revealed there. The same is true of the ark, the land, and the city of Jerusalem.

It is above all in this sense that the church is "holy"—not in the sense that its conduct is always pure, but in the sense that the Holy Spirit of God acts in it. To claim to make the church "holy" by our own good conduct is to usurp what belongs only to God.

The holiness of the church, precisely because it is the presence of God, does require a certain sort of conduct of its members. We cannot say that, since the holiness of the church is not our doing, our own obedience and purity are not important. Exactly the opposite is true: it is precisely because the holy God is present in the church that we, its members, must live in holiness.

It is important to remember that biblical holiness is much more than personal purity, and is not limited to our individual relationship with God. John Wesley correctly said that there is no holiness that is not social. Holiness is also a matter of our relationship with other people and with creation, of the manner in which we order and organize our social life.

(c) The church is catholic

Both the Nicene and the Apostles' Creeds refer to the church as "catholic." Since that word has become closely associated with a particular denomination, the Roman Catholic Church, many believers avoid using it, and therefore speak of the church as "universal." However, although the two words have similar meanings, there are important differences that must be taken into account.

In the most common use of the word, what is "universal" is to be found everywhere, with little or no variation. Thus we say, for instance, that the use of computers has become "universal," and by that we mean that anywhere in the world one can find computers, and that whoever knows how to use them in one place will also know how to use them in another. The same is true when we say that, as a result of economic globalization, English is becoming a universal language. Therefore, when we say that the church is "universal" we are saying that it is found throughout the world, and that it is the same everywhere. In that sense, the church has never been universal, and it is only in relatively recent times that it has even approached such an achievement. Therefore, it was not in that sense that the ancient creeds spoke of the church as "catholic."

During the first centuries of its existence, the church was present only in a band of land that extended from the British Isles in the north to Ethiopia in the south, and from the Iberian Peninsula on the west to India in the east. It did not arrive in China until the seventh century, and then it disappeared for some time. To America, Japan, and the Philippines it did not arrive until the sixteenth century, and to some regions of Africa and islands of the Pacific, it did not arrive until the nineteenth.

The original meaning of the term "catholic" refers not so much to universality in the sense of uniform extension as to inclusivity. The church is "catholic," not because it is everywhere, but because it includes all believers. In this sense, any church that claims to be the only one, excluding those who do not agree with it in every detail, would never be truly catholic, no matter how universal it might become.

Therefore, it was said that the witness of the four Gospels was "catholic" because it included the four different witnesses who are the four evangelists. Etymologically, the Greek word *catholikos* comes from the preposition *kata*, which means "according to," and from another word that means "all," "whole," "complete." The Gospel "according to Mark" is called in Greek *kata Markon*. That is why the ancient Christian writers refer to the four Gospels as the "catholic" witness to the gospel of Jesus—that is to say, the gospel according to the whole diversity of evangelists. Likewise, when the term "catholic" was first used to refer to the church (by Ignatius of Antioch, early in the second century) what this meant was that this church, in contrast to the Gnostic sects, did not depend on the supposed witness of a single apostle, or on some secret and particular teaching, but rather on the witness of all the apostles, even in their diversity. It was the church "according to the whole," or "according to all," and not according to a particular group.

The other significant dimension of the word "catholic" that is not included in "universal" is the temporal dimension. The church is catholic because it includes, not only the vast variety of believers and experiences of the present, but also those who have existed in centuries past. In other words, when we say that the church is catholic we are saying that the unity of which we spoke earlier also includes past generations through whom the witness to the gospel has reached us.

This is a dimension of the reality of the church that is often forgotten by those of us who live in modern times, especially those of us who are also Protestant. We imagine that the only true church is the one that exists today, and it is difficult for us to think that believers in past centuries belonged—and still belong—to the same church. It becomes even more difficult as we remember that in those times believers held doctrines that in many ways were different from ours, or that they followed practices that today are considered superstitious. However, without denying those differences, we must remember that it was precisely through such believers of centuries past that Scripture and the message of the gospel have reached us. If that was not a true church, our faith has reached us through unbelievers, and there were times when Jesus Christ had no witnesses in the world.

This leads us back to two other points mentioned above. The first is that the church is one, no matter how difficult it is for us to see this. Our church, if it is indeed the church of Jesus Christ, is the same church of Saint Augustine, of Saint Francis, of Martin Luther, of John Wesley, and of the millions of anonymous believers of centuries past. The second point is that we have to remember that there is always a significant distance between our doctrines and our theology on the one hand and God's reality on the other. Our doctrines, no matter how true, are not exact or final, but only partial and provisional, until the day when God's truth is revealed to us in its fullness.

Therefore, when we say that we believe in the "catholic church," we are affirming that we believe in that one church, Body of Christ, to which people from all times and places belong, all giving witness to the faith from their own perspective and place in history.

(d) The church is apostolic

The fourth of the signs, marks, or essential characteristics of the church that ancient creeds mention is that the church is "apostolic." This may be understood in three ways.

One way of understanding the apostolicity of the church is to claim that its leaders are the direct successors of the apostles. This is what is usually called "apostolic succession." Most of those who insist that the apostolicity of the church consists in its historical connection with the apostles understand that connection in this fashion.

As was said before, the insistence on "apostolic succession" began in the second century, where teachers appeared who taught strange doctrines—particularly Gnosticism—claiming that such doctrines were actually the secret teachings that Jesus had given to one of his disciples. Over against such claims, orthodox Christians pointed out that in the churches that the apostles had founded there were leaders or bishops who could show their direct connection with the apostles. At first this did not mean that all legitimate bishops had to be able to claim such a succession. It sufficed for their doctrine to be the same as that of those bishops who could claim it—the bishops of Antioch, Ephesus, Corinth, Rome, and so on. (In relatively recent times, many of the old traditions about the founding of several of those churches, and particularly about the uninterrupted succession of bishops, have been questioned by some historians. However, in the second century, when the argument of apostolic succession began to be employed, such traditions were generally accepted.)

The manner in which apostolic succession was understood evolved slowly. When in a city the church split, the bishop who could claim to be the successor of the previous bishop would use the principle of apostolic succession in order to support his legitimacy over against his opponent. Thus the notion arose that in order to be a bishop, or to be a properly ordained minister, one must form part of that uninterrupted chain of bishops who had succeeded one another from the times of the apostles.

It is thus that most of the churches that stress apostolic succession understand it today: in order to be an apostolic church, one must have bishops who are part of that unbroken line throughout the centuries. Others have held similar theories of apostolic succession, although without making it dependent on bishops. Thus, in much of the Reformed tradition—that is, the tradition evolving out of Zwingli and Calvin—it is understood that succession comes through an uninterrupted line of ministers. John Wesley, arguing that in the early church a bishop and a presbyter were the same, declared himself capable to transmit apostolic succession to others, even though he himself was not a bishop, but a presbyter.

A second way of understanding the apostolicity of the church has to do with doctrine and practice. In this case, the church is said to be apostolic because its doctrines and its practice are the same as those of the apostles. The church is apostolic because it believes what the apostles believed, because it worships as they did, and because it is organized as they organized the churches they founded. This way of understanding the apostolicity of the church existed from ancient times, parallel to the emphasis on apostolic succession that has just been discussed. However, it has been among Protestants, and especially among the groups that evolved significantly later than the Protestant Reformation of the sixteenth century, that this interpretation of apostolicity is most widespread.

Even a quick glimpse at history shows that there are difficulties with this way of understanding apostolicity. The doctrine and practices of every church have evolved, so that none is truly apostolic in this sense.

It is important to note that, although there are many Protestant churches that claim this sort of apostolicity, each of them insists in different aspects of what they consider to be "apostolic." Some declare themselves to be apostolic because they baptize only in the name of Jesus (Acts 8:16; 10:48; 19:5). Others declare themselves to be apostolic because they practice the commonality of goods (Acts 2:44-45; 4:32-35); others, because they kneel in order to pray (Acts 9:40; 20:36; 21:5), because women cover their heads (1 Cor. 11:5-6), or for some other similar reason. Many simply claim to be apostolic because their worship is spontaneous, without established rituals, or because the center of their worship is preaching.

The very variety of such claims shows the impossibility that a church can be truly "apostolic" in this sense. A church that does not live in the time of the apostles cannot live as they did. For example, in the churches of the apostles, the New Testament was not read, for it simply did not exist. Does this mean that in order to be "apostolic" we must cease reading the New Testament? Certainly not! Therefore, apostolicity in the sense of absolute identity between our doctrines and practices and those of the apostles is not possible, and frequently is connected to a simplistic view both of the apostolic church and of history.

This does not mean that the teachings of the apostles have lost their normative value. Certainly, the church is to uphold the teachings of the apostles. But it must always do this knowing that we are living in different times, and that such teachings have reached us through centuries that have both changed and enriched them.

A third way of understanding the apostolicity of the church is based on the etymology of the word *apostle*, which means "sent one." In this sense, the church is apostolic when it is sent, when it is missionary, when like the apostles it becomes an instrument of God's mission in the world. A church that ceases to be apostolic in this sense will not only die, but is already dead, for the life of the church is precisely in its being sent by God.

All of these ways of understanding apostolicity have something significant to contribute. If we limit ourselves to the first, apostolicity becomes mechanical and lacking in content. However, if we abandon it, we forget that, in one way or another, the fact that the gospel has reached our days is because of a long uninterrupted line—even though sometimes unknown to us—of witnesses who have brought it to our day.

If we limit ourselves to the second, apostolicity tends to be confused with details of doctrine or practice, and we reject the witness of that uninterrupted line of witnesses, declaring them to have been not truly "apostolic." However, if we forget this second sense, the witness of the apostles may well lose its normative value, and we run the risk of confusing the tradition that has reached us through centuries of evolution with the original message of the apostles.

If we limit ourselves to the third, we run the risk of a mission lacking in content and in historical continuity with the mission of the church through the centuries. Mission then becomes activism, going without knowing whither, doing without knowing why. However, if we set aside this third meaning, the church may well declare itself to be apostolic, but it will be like salt that has lost its flavor.

The church is apostolic for three reasons, all of them necessary: it is apostolic because it comes directly from the apostles. It is apostolic because it holds and proclaims the faith of the apostles. And it is apostolic because, like the apostles, it is sent in God's mission.

In summary, the church, that community of believers in Jesus Christ to which the New Testament refers with images such as "Body of Christ," is known because it is also one, holy, catholic, and apostolic.

This however does not say much unless it is expressed in the manner in which the church lives, both in its inner life and in its relationships with the world around it. This will be the subject of the next chapter.

VI. HOW DOES THE CHURCH LIVE?

Both the Apostles' and the Nicene Creed affirm that we believe "in the church." What do we mean by saying that we believe *in* the church? This does not mean only believing *that* the church exists, which could be affirmed by any person, even without being a believer. Nor does it mean that we believe *whatever the church says*, which would give the church an excessive authority. If the first is insufficient, the latter is too much. Believing *in* the church means that it is in the church, within it, as part of it, that we believe. We are believers because we are *in* the church, because it is as part of the church that we believe—just as when we say that we believe *in* God that does not mean only that we believe that God exists, but also and above all that our faith rests in God.

There is a certain paradox in this: we are in the church because we believe, but it is equally true that we believe because we are in the church. Unfortunately, modern individualism makes it difficult for us to see this second element of the paradox. We easily understand that we are in the church because we believe. If we did not believe, there would be no reason for us to be in the church. But it is also important to remember that the witness to faith has come to us, in one way or another, through the church—through that "catholic" church of which we spoke in the previous chapter, which has preserved and transmitted Scripture, and one of whose members somehow spoke to us for the first time of the gospel. Therefore, just as one must say that the egg comes from the chicken and the chicken from the egg, so must we say that we are in the church because we believe, and that we believe because

119

we are in the church. And, just as someone who insists in having only eggs, and has no interest in chickens, will eventually end up without chickens or eggs, thus any who claim to believe, but not *in* the church, will end up without church and without faith.

1. THE CHURCH LIVES BY THE WORD

Believing *in* the church means that our faith is nourished within the church. If the church is the Body of Christ, and we are its members, what keeps us alive is circulation and communication within that body—as what keeps a member of any body alive is the circulation of blood and the communication with the rest of the body through the nervous system. As Jesus told Satan in his temptations, it does not suffice to live by bread, for one also needs the Word of God (Matt. 4:4; Luke 4:4).

In this context it is important to remember what has been said before, that the Word of God is not only information or direction, but is also God's creative action. Just as when the darkness hears the Word speak, "let there be light," light leaps into existence, so too does the church exist and is constantly regenerated because in it the creative Word of God speaks—because that Word calls it into existence constantly, just as it still calls light out of darkness.

This Word of God is above all Jesus Christ, who is made present in the church through the Holy Spirit. But it is also Scripture, which in both Testaments witnesses to Jesus Christ. And even in a certain sense it is the proclamation of the Word that takes place in Christian worship.

As has already been stated, there is an enormous distance between the Word of God and any human word. Our words, no matter how much God uses them, remain human, and we must not claim that they are the Word of God. However, by God's grace, the words that we employ in our proclamation and witnessing become God's Word—not in the sense that we do not err, but rather in the sense that, even in the midst of our errors, God uses our words for creation and re-creation, creating and re-creating believers, creating and re-creating the church.

This proclamation of the church has taken different forms through the centuries. In the earliest times, when the church was still a small group and frequently persecuted, it was customary to gather very early on Sunday morning, before going to work, in order to spend hours listening to the reading and explanation of Scripture, and then celebrating the resurrection of the Lord by means of Communion. Thus it could be said that the service had two parts: the service of the word and the service of the table. Later, when the church became dominant, the worship service kept the same format: first the reading and exposition of Scripture and then Communion. During the Middle Ages, the first part of the service lost importance, to the point that it became common to celebrate mass (Communion) without preaching. The reformers of the sixteenth century, faced with the need to instruct the people on the Christian faith, and reacting to common practices in their time, insisted on the need for preaching whenever Communion was celebrated. At later times, several Protestant groups have carried that reaction to the other extreme, thinking that the center of worship is in preaching, and that Communion is to be celebrated only on special stated occasions. Sometimes it is thought that such preaching must be essentially evangelistic, for nonbelievers, and that the function of believers in worship is to pray for the conversion of the unbelievers who hear the sermon. In more recent times—beginning in the second half of the twentieth century—there has been a rapprochement of both extremes, so that in Roman Catholic churches there is more emphasis on preaching and in Protestant churches there is a tendency to celebrate Communion more frequently—in many cases, every Sunday, as was the practice in the ancient church.

2. THE WORD AND THE SACRAMENTS

Although it is true that when God speaks Word becomes action, it is also true that God speaks through actions—that is, that actions are also the Word of God.

Already in the second century, a Christian author, Justin Martyr, affirmed that God sometimes spoke by means of words, and other times by means of actions. Such actions, Justin and others called "types," because they were patterns showing the character and the will of God. We see throughout the Old Testament, and even in the New in the case of Elizabeth and John the Baptist, that a pattern is repeated of a barren woman who, by God's grace, gives birth to a child who is to be of great importance for the history of God's people. This "type" or pattern culminates in Mary, who because she is a virgin is the barren woman *par excellence,* giving birth to the most important person in the entire history of Israel and of humankind. The "type" or pattern of the barren woman is then a sign of the manner in which God's purposes are fulfilled even when human resources are insufficient, and that God's grace supplies what human nature cannot attain.

Later we shall see that the sacraments are rooted in other actions of God in the history of Israel, which are "types" or patterns of God's action. This is why Augustine says that the sacraments are the "visible word" of God.

Just as preaching, while being and remaining a human word, by God's grace becomes a channel for God's Word, so are there certain actions that the church has celebrated throughout the centuries, and through which it has experienced and heard the Word of God. These actions are usually called "sacraments."

If the church lives by the Word, the church needs both the verbal proclamation, whose central focus is the sermon, and the proclamation through action—the sacraments. This is why John Calvin affirms that "wherever we see the Word of God purely preached and heard, and the sacraments administered according to Christ's institution, we must not doubt that the church is present" (*Institutes,* 4.1.9).

(a) The sacraments in general

The word "sacrament" comes from the Latin *sacramentum,* which referred to the oath made by soldiers, and also to sacred things. Its use in the ancient church indicated both that what was taking place was holy, and that it was a covenant or oath among the participants—the believers as well as God. In the Greek-speaking church, the word used was *mysterion*—mystery.

According to an ancient definition dating as far back as Saint Augustine, a sacrament is "an external and visible sign of an inner and spiritual grace." To this the sixteenth-century reformers added the phrase "instituted by Christ," by which they limited their number to two: baptism and Communion—although some Anabaptist groups also count the washing of feet as a ritual instituted by Jesus (John 13:1-17).

In some Protestant circles, in reaction to Roman Catholic teachings regarding the sacraments and their efficacy, and in particular against interpretations that give the sacraments an almost magical character, the term "ordinance" is preferred to "sacrament." This emphasizes that they were ordered by Christ. However, the term "sacrament" does not imply any particular understanding of their nature or efficacy, and therefore there is no reason to reject it.

On the number of sacraments, there has never been agreement. In the ancient church baptism and Communion held a very special place, but many other things or rites that could serve as a channel for God's grace were also called "sacraments." Augustine speaks of more than thirty sacraments, and he includes among them such matters as making the sign of the cross and fasting. In the Middle Ages, Hugh of Saint Victor wrote a treatise *On the Sacraments of the Christian Faith* in which he shows that this wide use of the term was still current, even though he emphasizes the seven that eventually became the sacraments accepted by the Roman Catholic Church: baptism, confirmation, Communion, penance, extreme unction, marriage, and ordination. Some time later Peter Lombard, in the twelfth century, systematized the list of sacraments, limiting them to seven. This was done in his famous *Four Books of Sentences*, which soon became the basic textbook on theology for the entire Western church. Thus it was that the number of sacraments was eventually fixed at seven. The Second Council of Lyons, in 1274, declared that "the holy Roman church holds and teaches that the sacraments of the church are seven," and the same list was given.

The reformers, while accepting and confirming the value of practices and ceremonies such as marriage, ordination, and confession, refused to call them "sacraments," because they were not instituted by Jesus. Therefore, most Protestant churches affirm that there are two sacraments: baptism and Communion. However, as has been mentioned above, there are some churches that count the washing of feet as a sacrament. And there are others—particularly the Quakers or Friends—that refuse to celebrate any sacrament, insisting that such exterior means are not necessary for the inner experience of God's grace.

The fact that the sacraments are "visible signs" is important, because in a way the sacraments are an affirmation of the Christian doctrine of creation. From the early days of Christianity, and until this day, there have always been some who hold that only the spiritual is important, and that the material is either evil or at least of lesser importance. The sacraments, in using material elements such as water, bread, and wine, and affirming that these are visible signs of the invisible grace of God, remind us that all of creation is a sign of the grace of God and must be treated as such. To this we shall return later on in this chapter.

It is interesting to note that one of the sacraments, baptism, uses a substance that is found in its natural form throughout creation, whereas the other,

Communion, uses elements that are the result of human work. Water reminds us that creation is good. Bread and wine remind us of our responsibility of working jointly with God so that creation may be more productive.

The sacraments point not only to God's use of creation in order to bring us grace, but are also a sign and a reminder of God's use of history to the same end. The sacraments are rooted in the history of salvation, and root us in it.

Already in the ancient church, and throughout history, the sacraments have been seen as a continuation of the "types" or patterns of which Justin spoke, and which have always been an important aspect of biblical interpretation. This is true both of baptism and of Communion.

The water of baptism reminds us that God created the world amid the waters, that God saved Noah from among the waters, that God led Israel through the Red Sea and the river Jordan, gave the people water from the rock in the desert, rescued Jonah from the depths of the sea, and so on. Baptism itself, often called the "seal of faith," has also been compared with circumcision, which was the seal that God placed on the children of Israel as members of the people of God. Therefore, in celebrating this rite, we become a part of that entire history in which God has used water as a sign of salvation, and of that people whom God called in Abraham and Jacob.

Communion has always been interpreted in the light of the paschal supper and what it celebrates. Passover was the day in which the angel of the Lord smote the firstborn of Egypt, and thus achieved the liberation of Israel. This was what Jesus and his disciples were celebrating in the supper in which Jesus instituted Communion (Matt. 26:19; Mark 14:12; Luke 22:7-8). Throughout its history, Israel has celebrated this meal in memory of its liberation from Egypt. Throughout its history, the church has celebrated this meal in memory of its liberation from sin and death through the death and resurrection of Jesus.

Also, both baptism and Communion point toward the future that God has promised. Baptism is not only a sign of the death of Christ, but also of resurrection with him (Rom. 6:4; Col. 2:12); and the water of baptism also points to the future Jerusalem, through which runs "the river of the water of life, bright as crystal" (Rev. 22:1). Likewise, in celebrating Communion "in remembrance" of Jesus, we remember not only his passion, death, and resurrection, but also his promise to be with us in order to drink anew of the fruit of the vine (Matt. 26:29; Mark 14:25; Luke 22:16; 1 Cor. 11:26).

One of the most ancient prayers that has been preserved for the celebration of Communion (in the *Didache*, which probably dates from late in the first century or early in the second), includes this future dimension: "As this bread was dispersed over the mountains, and has been gathered into one, so may your church be gathered from the ends of the earth in your kingdom."

The efficacy of the sacraments has been widely discussed. When we say, as did Augustine, that a sacrament is "a visible and external sign of an inner and spiritual grace," what do we really mean? Is the sacrament only a sign of something that happens quite apart from it? Or is it, on the contrary, a vehicle through which God effects that "inner and spiritual grace"? On these matters there has been much discussion, and some have held quite extreme positions—from some medieval writers, who claim for the sacraments an almost magical efficacy, to some modern Protestants, for whom the sacrament is no more than a way of remembering what we already know.

What makes a sacrament valid and efficacious? Again, on this there have been and still are enormous differences of opinion. According to traditional Roman Catholic doctrine, the sacrament acts *ex opere operato*, that is, by its own efficacy. At the other extreme, there are Protestants who affirm that the efficacy of the sacrament depends entirely on the faith of the person who receives it, and even sometimes on the character and the faith of the one administering it. Whereas the first position seems to discount the importance of faith in the sacraments, the second seems to turn the sacrament into an accomplishment of our faith, rather than a manifestation or instrument of God's grace.

These questions have been posed about each of the sacraments. Regarding baptism, the ancient church had to deal with the question of whether a baptism administered by heretics was valid. Some, such as Cyprian in the third century and Athanasius in the fourth, held that such baptism could not be valid, and that therefore those who had been baptized by heretics, if they returned to the Orthodox Church, should be rebaptized. Basil of Caesarea, in the fourth century, distinguished between heretics—that is, those who held false teachings—and schismatics—those who simply had withdrawn from the rest of the church. According to Basil, a baptism performed by heretics is not valid, but one performed by schismatics is. However, from the pastoral point of view, this did not resolve the problem, for if baptism depends on the orthodoxy of the one administering it, one never knows whether one has really been baptized, since it is impossible to know with absolute certainty what a minister thinks or believes. In extreme cases, this would lead believers to repeat their baptism as often as possible, in order to make certain that at least one of them is valid. We know of people who have decided to be re-baptized because they have later discovered that the person baptizing them was living in adultery, or because they have met another minister who seemed holier than the previous one. For that reason, slowly the view became prevalent that baptism, as long as it is administered with water and in the name of the Father, the Son, and the Holy Spirit, is valid, and is not to be repeated. Such is to this day the official position of the Roman Catholic Church and of most of the older Protestant churches.

Something similar happened with reference to ordination, sometimes considered a sacrament. Repeatedly, but especially in North Africa beginning in the fourth century, the question was posed of whether an ordination administered by unworthy persons was valid. In North Africa, when the persecution of Christians ceased in the fourth century, there were some who claimed that the bishops who had not remained firm throughout the persecution were unworthy, that any receiving Communion with them became unworthy, and that any person ordained by them or by their successors was not truly ordained. It eventually became necessary to decide also that ordination does not depend on the virtue of the one performing it, for in that case one would never know whether a minister is properly ordained or not—and therefore whether the sacraments that the people receive from such a minister are valid.

Similar considerations regarding Communion, marriage, and so on, led the medieval church to affirm that the sacraments have their own efficacy, *ex opere operato*. This became the official doctrine of the Roman Catholic Church in the Council of Trent in the sixteenth century—although the Council noted that the sacrament is efficacious only if the one receiving it offers no hindrance.

The reformers of the sixteenth century rejected such teachings. Luther insisted that sacraments without faith are useless (although, as we shall see, he did believe that infants should be baptized). Calvin declares that the doctrine according to which the sacraments confer grace, as long as no mortal sin hinders them (that is, the doctrine of *ex opere operato* as defined by the Council of Trent) is "pestilent and fatal," in that "in promising justification without faith it propels souls towards damnation." (*Institutes* 4.14.14) These reformers also opposed the doctrine that what makes the sacrament effective is our faith. On the contrary, the sacraments are God's actions before being ours. Their efficaciousness is in that they carry the Word of God and its promise of salvation. Since the Word of God is active and creative, in the sacraments that Word acts for our salvation. Therefore, although sacraments without faith are useless, what gives them efficacy is not our faith, but the grace of God acting in them.

In summary, in considering the sacraments one must take care not to attribute to them a magical efficacy, as if by the mere fact of celebrating a rite we could control God's grace. However, at the same time we must affirm that God acts in them, and that therefore they are not reduced to an expression of our faith or to a spiritual exercise on our part. This helps us understand both baptism and Communion.

(b) Baptism

According to the Gospel of Matthew, the last commission Jesus gave his disciples was to go and make disciples, "baptizing them in the name of the Father and of the Son and of the Holy Spirit" (Matt. 28:19). Thus, from its very beginning the church has practiced baptism as a rite or sacrament by which new believers are initiated into the church. Except for a few groups such as the Quakers or Friends, all Christian churches affirm and practice baptism. However, in spite of the almost universal practice of baptism, there are great disagreements regarding it. These disagreements revolve mainly around two points at issue: the *manner* in which baptism is to be celebrated, and whether only those are to be baptized whose *age* is sufficient for them to confess their faith—that is, whether infants are to be baptized or not.

The discussion regarding the manner in which baptism is to be celebrated deals principally with whether it must be by immersion, or whether it can also be practiced by pouring or by sprinkling water over the head. On this matter, historians generally agree in that in ancient times the most common form of practicing baptism was to "descend to the waters," and that the practice of baptizing only the head is generally much later—although from a very early date it was accepted in exceptional cases.

The *Didache*, that ancient document which has already been mentioned, offers instructions for baptism. It says that baptisms should normally be performed in "living water"—that is, running water, such as a river. However, apparently the place in which the *Didache* was written—probably the desert of Syria—did not have water in abundance, and therefore it goes on to say that if living water is not available, "other water"—that is, a pond or reservoir—may also be used; and that if such water is not available, baptism may be performed by pouring water over the head three times, "in the name of the

Father, and the Son, and the Holy Ghost." The most ancient baptismal fonts that have been found are sufficiently capacious so that the rite can be celebrated in the water. However, they are rather shallow, which suggests that the person knelt in the water, and then had water poured over the head.

By the fourth century, it became a common practice to baptize those who were already on their deathbeds by placing water on their heads. But baptism by immersion, or at least by kneeling in the water while more water was poured over the head, continued being the norm. When Arianism became a threat to the Western church, certain councils decreed that baptism should be done with a single immersion, in order to signal the unity of the three divine persons—however, that very decision shows that immersion was still the common practice.

It was well into the Middle Ages, with the conversion of the Scandinavians and other Northern people whose climate was bitterly cold, that baptism by placing water on the head became common. In Rome, children continued being baptized by immersion at least into the twelfth century. The Eastern churches still baptize children and adults in like manner.

Therefore, there is no doubt that baptism by pouring or sprinkling water on the head, even though it was always an acceptable alternative, was not the normal manner in which it was performed. This is why many churches that until recently only practiced baptism in this manner have now begun to make provision for baptism, either by immersion, or by kneeling in the water and having more water poured over the head.

At any rate, the question of the manner in which baptism is to be administered, even though sometimes bitterly debated among Christians, is of less importance than the age at which baptism may be received. On this matter, historians can be of less help, for there is no consensus among scholars regarding the practice in the ancient church.

There are several texts that can be quoted to support the baptism of infants, and others that can be quoted against it. The fact is that none of these texts— or even all of them together—suffice to prove one position or the other. "Pedobaptists" (those who baptize children) refer to Acts 16:33, where we are told about the jailer in Philippi, that "he and his entire family were baptized," as a sign that whole families, including children, were baptized. But the opposite side argues that there is no proof that the jailer had small children. It is not until well into the second century, in the writings of Hippolytus, that there is specific mention of "children" who are to be baptized—and in this case they are clearly children who are not old enough to answer for themselves. There are not many texts arguing that children should not be baptized;

and those that exist, mostly from the third century, offer very different reasons than those adduced today against the baptism of infants. Whereas the argument today is that infants who have no use of reason cannot have faith and therefore cannot be baptized, the argument adduced at that point was that children still had not committed all the sins of youth, and therefore their baptism should be postponed!

Theologically, both positions regarding infant baptism have solid arguments. On the one hand, those who oppose it argue that in order for baptism to be valid one must have faith. Since infants cannot even understand the message of the gospel, much less accept it, they must not be baptized. On the other hand, those who baptize infants say that this very act is a sign of the primacy of grace, a sign that God acts in us, not because we do something or believe something, but simply because God loves us. It is God's love that makes us believe, and not vice versa—that is, our belief does not make God love us. At any rate, this is a debate that will probably continue for some time, and in which probably the best advice is for each side to listen to the other and appreciate the value of what it is saying.

It should be added that the matter of infant baptism has implications that go beyond baptism itself. In general, those churches that insist on adult baptism tend to emphasize the distinction between the civil community and the church, while churches that see themselves as practically coextensive with the society in which they exist tend to practice infant baptism.

What is the significance of baptism? On this there is a measure of agreement among Christians from various churches and times, although there are significant differences of emphasis. What one most often hears in Protestant churches is that baptism is a witness. It is a witness given by those being baptized, who thus announce their faith. It is a witness that God gives us of divine love, allowing us to die to the old life and be born to new life. It is a witness of the covenant between God and God's people, and of God's promise that this people will be redeemed. Also, baptism is a washing. The "inner and spiritual grace" of which baptism is an "outer and visible sign" is the grace that washes us from sin. What one does not hear as frequently today, but which is also true and has been a traditional doctrine of the church from the most ancient times, is that baptism is a grafting. By baptism we are grafted into the church, which is the Body of Christ—therefore, by baptism we are grafted into Christ and become partakers of his life.

This last point is important, for it implies that baptism is effective throughout life, and is not only the beginning of Christian life. During the Middle Ages, the notion that baptism was a washing away of earlier sins left open the question of what is to be done with sins committed after baptism. This in turn led to the development of the entire penitential system of the Roman Catholic Church. If baptism is a washing, any later stain must be washed by other means—in this case, confession and penance, or, in the early church, the "second baptism in blood" of martyrdom. If baptism is a grafting, it is valid and effective throughout life. When a branch is grafted into the vine— or, in modern medicine, when an organ is grafted into a body—that branch lives out of its constant connection with the vine, of the sap that flows from the roots and which nourishes it. Likewise, if baptism is a grafting into the Body of Christ, it is valid whenever, thanks to that graft, the life of Christ flows in us. Both major reformers, Luther and Calvin, affirm that baptism holds its power in us through faith in the promises given by God in our baptism.

Finally, an often forgotten point must be emphasized: baptism is a communal sacrament. It is not only a matter of the believer, the person performing the rite, and God. It is an act involving the entire church, which now receives a new member—as a vine receives a new branch. In baptism, not only the person receiving the sacrament makes vows, but also the entire community vows to safeguard and nourish the new member.

(c) Communion

Just as Jesus instructed his disciples to baptize, so did he institute Communion or the Lord's Supper in that last supper when, just before being arrested, he told his disciples: "Do this in remembrance of me." And, just as baptism had its roots in the history of Israel, so does Communion have similar roots in the paschal meal, in the manna descending from heaven, and in the promise of the final banquet.

Throughout history, Communion has been the center of Christian worship. The main exception, which is relatively recent, has been the case of a number of Protestant churches that, reacting against magical and superstitious interpretations of Communion, and seeing the need to educate the people, have placed the sermon at the center of worship, and have relegated Communion to an occasional celebration.

The history of Communion is long and complex. However, a brief outline of some of the highlights may be useful.

There is every indication that in the very early times of the church what was celebrated was a community meal in which people shared what they brought, although the bread and the cup were always at the center of the celebration. Such a meal, besides being a memorial of the death and resurrection of Jesus, was also a foretaste of the final banquet, where there would be abundance and none would want. This is why in 1 Corinthians Paul shows such outrage because some go to this meal in order to be sated and drunk with what they take, while others do not have enough to eat. As Paul says, this is "not to discern the body of Christ," that is, to forget that those who are present are the Body of Christ, all members of one another.

Soon, however, Communion was limited to what had always been its two essential elements: the bread and the wine. This was probably due to a series of practical considerations as well as to the difficulty of having an entire meal in common, especially when the church was growing or under persecution. (It is interesting to note that both in baptism and in Communion there was a tendency to reduce matters to their minimal expression: in baptism, by baptizing only the head; and in Communion, by limiting it to a bit of bread and wine.)

During the early centuries, Communion was mostly a celebration. Although in it the passion of Jesus was remembered, his resurrection and impending return were also remembered and celebrated. This is why Communion was celebrated on the first day of the week, the day of the resurrection of the Lord, and not normally on Friday, the day of his death. It was early in the Middle Ages that Communion began taking the funereal tones that in many churches is still retained today. (However, in the second half of the twentieth century a movement of liturgical renewal, based on the ancient liturgies of the second and third centuries, began returning Communion to its original celebrative character.)

Throughout the centuries, there have been many controversies about Communion. The most continued subject of debate, even to this day, has to do with the presence of Christ in Communion. To this we shall return. However, at least two other controversies should be mentioned.

One of these arose from the custom of giving the laity only the bread, and reserving the chalice for the clergy. This custom, which arose in western Europe during the Middle Ages, was probably based on a profound sense of awe before the presence of Christ in the bread and the wine, and the dreadful possibility of spilling the latter. It eventually became the generally accepted practice throughout the Western church. A protest against that practice was one of the main issues of the followers of John Huss called "Utraquists," which means that they insisted in the sacrament being offered to all "in both *(utraque)* kinds." The Protestants of the sixteenth century also insisted on Communion in both kinds. Eventually, as a consequence of the Second Vatican Council, the Roman Catholic Church allowed the ancient practice of communion in both kinds.

Another controversy, this time between the Eastern and Western churches, had to do with the bread to be used in Communion. In the Western church it became customary to celebrate Communion with unleavened bread (as is the traditional host of Roman Catholicism). For Eastern Christians, this was tantamount to confusing the Christian celebration with the Jewish Passover, which was celebrated with unleavened bread. For a long time this developed into bitter debates between East and West. Today, at least in the West, few show much concern about whether the bread is leavened or not.

Communion, which ought to be the bond of union among believers, is unfortunately one of the main points of discord among various Christian traditions. Although there are other issues involved, the main point under discussion has been the presence of Christ in the sacrament—or rather, the *manner* of that presence, for all agree that Christ is present. On this matter, there is a wide gamut of opinions, from the doctrine of transubstantiation held by Roman Catholicism to those at the other extreme who hold that Communion is merely a memorial act in which Christ is present because we remember him, or if not, an act that allows us to remember that Christ is already present.

The doctrine of transubstantiation was not an official doctrine of the Church of Rome until the year 1215, when the Fourth Lateran Council declared that in the eucharistic celebration the bread and the wine are "transubstantiated" into the Body and Blood of the Lord. But similar opinions were circulating in the church long before. Already in the fourth century there were those who carried a bit of consecrated bread hanging from their necks, as an amulet. Shortly thereafter, Augustine affirmed both that the bread and the wine "signify" the Body and Blood of Christ, and that they "are" that Body and Blood—which is an indication that at the time the matter was not being debated, and that therefore it was not necessary to cross all the t's, as it was later.

In the ninth century there was a controversy over similar issues, that is, whether the presence of the Body and the Blood of Christ in communion is such that what one's eyes see is really that body and blood, or is it rather a matter of faith, which can only be seen by the eyes of faith. In the same context there were debates as to whether the body of Christ present in the sacrament is the same that is seated at the right hand of God the Father. In the midst of that controversy, there were those who claimed that the presence of the Body of Christ in Communion was not "in truth," but only "in figure." Toward the end of that century, the opposite opinion was expressed in terms that came very close to the later doctrine of transubstantiation: "It is a pestilent madness for the faithful to doubt that the substance of the bread and the wine placed upon the altar become the Body and Blood of Christ through the mystery of the priest and thanksgiving, and that God does this through his divine grace and secret power." (Haymo of Halberstadt *De Corppre et Sanguine Domini*) The controversy, although having seemingly ended, appeared again in the eleventh century, and then again and again throughout the history of the church. Although the definition of the Fourth Lateran Council practically ended the controversy within Roman Catholicism, the issue reappeared with the Protestant Reformation and some of its forerunners.

According to the doctrine of transubstantiation, when the bread and the wine are consecrated their substance disappears, and their place is taken by the substance of the Body and Blood of Christ. Since what is transformed is the substance, and not the accidents, the bread still tastes like bread, smells like bread, and so forth; but in truth, it has become the Body of Christ.

This doctrine was rejected by the Protestant reformers of the sixteenth century, even though they did not all agree as to the exact manner in which Christ is present in Communion. Among the main reformers, Luther held that the body of Jesus was physically and really present in the elements, which, however, continue being what they were before. This is what some have called the doctrine of "consubstantiation," although Luther never gave it that name. At the other end, some of the Anabaptists claimed that the sacrament was only a symbol of something that took place in the inner self—and some even suggested that there was no reason to celebrate it. Ulrich Zwingli, the main Swiss reformer before Calvin, held a position similar to that of some Anabaptists, for he said that Communion is a sign or witness to the faith that believers offer the church and even themselves. Calvin took an intermediate stance, declaring that Christ is really present in Communion, but not physically in the sense that the body of Christ descends from heaven, but spiritually, in the sense that in Communion those who partake in it are taken to heaven, to the presence of Christ, and there enjoy a foretaste of the final banquet.

The disagreement between Luther and Zwingli on this point was clear and firm. When the two reformers met at Marburg in order to settle their differences, they were able to agree on all points except this one. Luther insisted that the words of Jesus, "this is my body," should be taken literally, while Zwingli held that they really meant "this represents my body." At the end of the colloquy, Luther declared, "We are not of the same spirit."

Calvin expressed his opinions especially in his famous work, *Institutes of the Christian Religion*, whose first edition Luther read and approved. But after Luther's death, as Calvin continued elaborating his position, there were Lutherans who began saying that it was radically different from that of Luther, and not acceptable. Although some were more moderate, the followers of the two great reformers progressively grew apart theologically—on this point as well as on others—and already by the seventeenth century the debates between Lutherans and Calvinists were as bitter as the debates between Protestants and Catholics. From that point on, one of the characteristic traits of the Lutheran tradition has been its insistence on the real and physical presence of the Body of Christ in Communion.

This does not mean, however, that for Luther and his followers the bread is still the Body of Christ after the act of Communion is finished and the congregation disperses—as it is in the Roman Catholic tradition, where it is held that the bread is still the Body of Christ, and must be reserved and treated as such.

In more recent times, such debates have become less strident, as each Christian tradition is enriched with what it learns from the others. Although transubstantiation is still the official doctrine of the Roman Catholic Church, in many Catholic masses there is much less talk about that than about Communion as a bond of unity among believers, or as a celebration of the life, death, resurrection, and return of Jesus. Likewise, there are fewer and fewer Protestants who insist that Communion is only a rite like any other, whose value is simply in that it reminds us of Jesus.

This is partly due, as in the case of baptism, to the manner in which many churches have gone back to ancient traditions regarding Communion—traditions that are much older than the debates that have just been summarized. Both in Catholic worship and in the worship of many Protestant churches, a number of practices from the early centuries of the life of the church have been restored. As part of that restoration, the sense of celebration and joy in

Communion is being recovered, and the stress lies once again on Communion as a sign of our shared life as the Body of Christ. This in turn has restored to Communion its original communitary character, as a celebration, not of the individual or for private devotion, but rather of the community of faith.

One of the points on which the reformers rejected medieval practice was the celebration of private masses, in which the priest was by himself as he consecrated and consumed the elements. The communitarian dimension of communion goes against such practices.

All of this poses once again the matter of the meaning of Communion. In the Middle Ages, and later in the official doctrine of the Roman Catholic Church, it was thought that Communion was the repetition of the sacrifice of Christ—although a bloodless sacrifice—which therefore conferred merit. Hence the custom of "saying mass" for souls in purgatory. Protestants rejected this way of understanding the efficacy of Communion, and the more radical among Protestants, especially those who had been more influenced by modernity and its rationalism, came to the point of thinking that what was important in Communion was only the spiritual exercise performed by the believer, remembering the passion of Christ and the believer's own sin that required such a sacrifice. Today, there is a tendency to emphasize what was also one of the most common themes in the ancient church: Communion as a means whereby the members who have been grafted into the Body of Christ are nourished from that body. If baptism is like a grafting, Communion is the sap or the blood that runs from the body to the grafted member, keeping it alive. That is why many ancient Christian writers affirm that whoever withdraws from Communion withdraws from Jesus.

In this context it is important to point out that in the ancient church Communion and worship were practically the same. It was not meant that what nourished the faith of the members grafted into the body was specifically or only the bread and the wine, but rather the participation in the total act of worship and Communion.

What all of this implies is that Communion, like baptism, is a communal celebration. It is not the manner in which the individual believer approaches Christ or obtains grace, but rather the manner in which the community as a whole—and therefore each individual believer—is nourished and lives.

(d) The world as a sacrament

At the beginning of this chapter it was stated that for a long time Christians spoke of all sorts of rites and practices as "sacraments," and that although baptism and Communion were always central in Christian worship, it was only much later that the number of sacraments began to be limited and defined. This is partly because if, as stated at the beginning of this book, the world and all that exists in it are God's creation and reflect their creator, then the entire world is sacramental in nature.

The two sacraments themselves remind us of the world. Baptism, with its water, reminds us of the world of nature, in which water plays such an important role. Communion, with its bread and its wine, reminds us of the world of human industry, which takes the elements of nature—wheat and grapes—and gives them new form and new value. Both lead to God, creator and sustainer of the natural world, as well as of the world that human labor creates. In the ancient church, it was sometimes pointed out that baptism was a sign of the beginning of the redemption of creation by building octagonal baptismal fonts: this was the point at which the eighth day of creation, that is, the reign of God, began. Likewise, in Communion not only the death of Jesus for the sins of believers was remembered, but also his return in glory, to reign over the world. Both baptism and Communion have cosmic dimensions, reminding us that the entire cosmos is God's creation, and that God not only made it, but continues loving it. This in turn means that the manner in which we live in the present world is of great significance—it has, so to speak, sacramental value. As we saw in discussing the doctrine of creation, our stewardship requires that we deal with creation with respect and with love. The same stewardship requires that we deal with one another—not only among Christians, but among all humankind—with respect and with love.

In the Second Vatican Council, the phrase "the sacrament of the neighbor," was used. This does not mean that the Roman Church is considering the possibility of adding a new sacrament to the seven traditional ones. What it means is that the neighbor has sacramental value. In the Gospel of Matthew, Jesus tells us that those who serve the needy serve him (Matt. 25:34-40). Therefore, it does not suffice to speak about the presence of Christ in Communion; we also have to speak about the presence of Christ in the needy, who thereby become a sacrament to us.

This is the basis for Christian ethics, which is not limited to the purely personal, but extends also to the social. Ethics is not an appendix or supplement to Christian life and theology, but is rather part of theology and is essential for Christian life. If it is not discussed more fully in this small book, that is because its importance is such that in most theological curricula it is studied as a separate discipline.

In short, the physical world, as God's creation, and all human beings, as creatures of God, have a sacramental value for believers. Thus, just as the ancients said repeatedly that whoever withdraws from baptism and Communion withdraws from Christ, so does whoever withdraws from the world and the neighbor withdraws from Christ.

VII. WHAT IS OUR HOPE?

These days, one can hardly move without hearing about the "last times"—or, in more technical terms, "eschatology."

The word *eschatology* comes from two Greek roots. One means "last" or "final." The other is the same as is found in the word *theology*, and means "study, treatise, discourse, doctrine, or science." Therefore, in theology the doctrine of the last things is called "eschatology."

The movie and book industries profit from the curiosity and fear of their audiences in order to create and sell fantastic stories about cataclysmic events, Antichrists, and the final destruction of the world. This is to be expected, since the purpose of such industries is to make a profit, and they have discovered that such subjects are popular. However, what is sadly disconcerting is to hear from so many pulpits, as well as from radio and television preachers, and even in our Sunday schools, sermons, and classes about these subjects that seem to be more a matter of science fiction than of biblical faith. It would seem that there are preachers and teachers who believe that the best way of preaching the love of God is to scare their audiences! Or at least it would seem that they are attempting to compete with the sensationalism of Hollywood.

What motivates such preachers and teachers is not only sensationalism or curiosity, but an entire theological tradition in many of our churches, quite widespread among the people, which leans in that direction. This tendency is largely caused by the impact of

Dispensationalism on North American culture, and through American missionaries on the rest of the world.

Dispensationalism is a doctrine that divides the interventions of God in history in a series of seven periods or "dispensations." Each of these dispensations is distinguished by a specific revelation of God, to which humankind does not respond in obedience, with the ensuing judgment and punishment from God. Although throughout history the subject of "dispensations" has appeared repeatedly in Christian theology, this has usually not led to an entire scheme of human history, or to predictions regarding the future. It was in the twentieth century that modern Dispensationalism appeared in the work of John Nelson Darby, who systematized it into a scheme culminating in the "rapture," and in which we were told that we are now in a sort of parentheses or dispensation that is called "the age of the Church." All of this Darby joined with his premillennialism.

The doctrine of the "millennium" is based almost exclusively on the twentieth chapter of Revelation, whose first verses speak of "a thousand years." On the basis of these verses, those who take them literally debate whether the "rapture" of the church is to occur before that millennium ("premillennialism") or after ("postmillennialism").

According to Darby's scheme, we are now in the dispensation of the church, which he also calls "of Grace," which began with the resurrection of Christ and will end with the "great tribulation" (which he bases on Matthew 24:21 and Revelation 7:14). After that great tribulation will come the return of Christ, the millennium, the confrontation between good and evil, Armageddon, and the final judgment. For these reasons, Darby's scheme is called "premillennialist dispensationalism."

That sort of dispensationalism became popular thanks to the Scofield Bible, published in 1909. That Bible, by combining verses from various parts of Scripture, offers an entire scheme of the various "dispensations." It is popular because it reads the entire Bible—especially Daniel and Revelation—as a great mystery or puzzle that can only be understood with Scofield's notes. Since this is a similar approach to that of occultism and the Cabala, it has become very attractive at a time in which such doctrines are increasingly popular. Whoever has a Bible with such notes imagines to have discovered a mystery hidden throughout the centuries, and only recently solved by Scofield's keys.

Sadly, all of this hides the richness and the joy of eschatology, turning it into a matter of predicting the future, or of discovering at what stage of the final events we now find ourselves. In truth, the subject of eschatology is hope—a hope based on what God has done in Jesus Christ, what God continues doing through the Holy

Spirit, and what God will do in the reign of glory. Therefore, although hope is always directed toward the future, eschatology is not limited in its implications to that which is to happen, but is based on what has happened and has implications for our present lives. If eschatology is limited to guessing when and how the end will come, it has lost its joy and its true nature as the doctrine of Christian hope.

When speaking of "hope," it is necessary to clarify what is meant by that word. There are indeed different sorts of hope, and most of them are quite different from Christian hope. Sports fans hope that their team will win, but that hope is usually little more than a wish. Those who study for exams hope to obtain good grades. That hope may be a wish that is, however, based on facts as well as effort. But neither the hope of having one's team win, nor the hope of making a good grade, is certain. In contrast, when one speaks of Christian hope one does not mean that it is possible or even probable that something will take place, but rather that one is certain that it will be so. One often hears that the only two sure things in life are death and taxes. Christian hope is even surer than death itself—indeed, it overcomes death. That is why 1 Peter 1:3 calls this "a living hope through the resurrection of Jesus Christ from the dead, and . . . an inheritance that is imperishable." That is to say, our hope is grounded on the actions and promises of the God who does not lie. In the same vein, Hebrews 6:19 says that "we have this hope, a sure and steadfast anchor of the soul, a hope that enters the inner shrine behind the curtain."

1. HOPE SEEKING UNDERSTANDING

It has been said that, just as theology is faith seeking understanding, so is eschatology "hope seeking understanding." In 1 Peter 3:15 we are told "Always be ready to make your defense to anyone who demands from you an accounting for the hope that is in you." This "accounting for the hope" is the purpose of eschatology. It is not predicting the future. It is not to intimidate unbelievers—note that 1 Peter tells us that we are to do this "with gentleness and reverence" (1 Pet. 3:16). Nor is the purpose of eschatology to give us hope. The hope comes from elsewhere. What eschatology does is help us give an accounting of the hope by which we live.

It is not by coincidence that Paul relates hope with faith and love: "Now faith, hope, and love abide" (1 Cor. 13:13). He does the same in Romans 5:1-5, where he begins speaking of faith, then turns to how suffering leads to hope, and hope does not disappoint, "because God's love has been poured into our hearts." Christian faith is nourished on the unshakable hope that God, the God of love, will not disappoint us. Therefore, to speak of Christianity is to speak of the hope that stands at its very heart. Without hope there is no faith; and without faith, there is no Christian hope.

If part of the function of theology is to critique the life and proclamation of the church in the light of the gospel, then part of the function of eschatology is to critique the proclamation of the church regarding the future in the light of Christian hope. Just as theology does not claim to penetrate the divine mystery, but speaks only in terms of what God has chosen to reveal, so eschatology does not seek to penetrate the mysteries of the future, or to "know the times or periods that the Father has set by his own authority" (Acts 1:7). The function of eschatology is to help the church and believers give an accounting of their hope, and to live out of that hope.

2. CHRIST, OUR HOPE

Now, then, what is our hope? According to the biblical witness, the correct answer is not so much a "what" as a "who." The biblical answer is that the Lord Jesus Christ is our hope (1 Tim. 1:1); "Christ in you, the hope of glory" (Col. 1:27). Christ, our hope, has healed the rupture between humankind and God that sin had caused, and thus the possibility of life eternal in God's company becomes a reality (Rom. 5:10-11; Col. 1:22). The text from Hebrews 6:19-20 goes on to say that our hope "enters the inner shrine behind the curtain, where Jesus, a forerunner on our behalf, has entered." It is the resurrection of Jesus from among the dead that makes our own resurrection possible. Christ is the anchor of our faith, the rock on which our hope is grounded. It is by reason of that hope that we know we shall not be disappointed. In this, we continue along the line of the faith of Israel, which affirms that God is the hope of

Israel, and that all who forsake God shall be put to shame (Jer. 17:13), whereas those whose hope is in God shall be happy and blessed (Ps. 146:5). Furthermore, such hope is not something we can have by ourselves, but is rather something given to us "by the power of the Holy Spirit" (Rom. 15:13). "For through the Spirit, by faith, we eagerly wait for the hope of righteousness" (Gal. 5:5). Paul knew full well that hope and trust in the promises of God, especially in times of trials and difficulties, is not something we can produce within ourselves, but is rather something that comes to us through the sustaining power of the Holy Spirit in our lives and our churches—for Christian hope is not purely individual, but is also communal, a gift of the Spirit to the church.

This power of the Spirit allows us to trust patiently in the fulfillment of what we do not yet see: "For in hope we were saved. Now hope that is seen is not hope. For who hopes for what is seen? But if we hope for what we do not see, we wait for it with patience" (Rom. 8:24-26).

This patient but hopeful awaiting is the very essence of faith—again, without hope it is impossible to have faith.

On affirming that our hope is Jesus Christ, we are also saying that what we expect is not an unknown. Even though the individual death of each of us, as well as the final consummation of history, still holds for us mysteries we cannot penetrate, those mysteries do not cause us to be afraid, for we know that beyond them we are being awaited by the one who already came to be with us, whom we already know and serve by the power of the Holy Spirit: Jesus Christ, the conqueror of death and Lord of history. The one who comes is the one who has already come; the one whom we expect is the same whom we already know. Therefore, Christian hope not only helps us live today, but allows us to live as those who do not fear the morrow—as those who know that beyond the threshold of death we shall be met by Life itself, Jesus our Lord and Savior.

Meanwhile, while we wait for him, we are not alone. Jesus himself promised that, during his absence, the Comforter, the Holy Spirit, would be with us. Paul repeatedly refers to the Spirit as the "first installment" of the promise (see 2 Cor. 1:22; 5:5; also Eph. 1:13-14: "the promised Holy Spirit; this is the pledge of our inheritance").

3. THE REIGN OF GOD

If the answer to the question, Who is our hope? is Jesus Christ, the answer to the other question, How do we describe our hope? is the reign of God.

The reign of God is repeatedly mentioned in Scripture, where we are told once and again that the reign is the content of the preaching of Jesus and of the gospel. Both the preaching of Jesus and the preaching of the early church are "the gospel of the reign of God" (Mark 1:14; Luke 4:43; 8:1; 9:2, 11; Acts 1:3; 8:12; 19:8; 20:25; 28:23, 31). In the Gospel of Luke alone, the phrase "reign of God" appears thirty-two times. Repeatedly, as an introduction to his parables, Jesus says, "To what shall I compare the reign of God?" which means that these parables are teachings not simply about common human life—or even about religious life—but about the reign of God (Matt. 11:16; Luke 13:18, 20).

A similar phrase that needs clarification is "the reign of heaven" or "the kingdom of heaven." That phrase appears only in the Gospel of Matthew, who uses it thirty-two times. Almost every time that Luke says "the reign of God," Matthew says "the reign of heaven." This does not mean that Matthew wishes to emphasize the "spiritual" or "celestial" nature of the reign. Matthew does this because among some Jews every effort was made not to speak directly about God, thus seeking to fulfill the commandment of not taking the name of God in vain. Thus sometimes instead of saying "God" one referred to "the throne," or "heaven." (This is why sometimes the book of Revelation, instead of saying "God," says "the one that was seated on the throne.") Therefore, what Matthew means by the phrase "reign of heaven" is the same as what the other Gospels mean by the "reign of God."

The hope for a "day of the LORD," and for a new order in which the will of God will be made fully manifest, appears constantly in Scripture. That is the hope of the people upon leaving Egypt. It is their hope upon entering the promised land; it is the reason the prophets challenge the injustices of the established order; it is the vision of prophets during the exile; in short, it is the hope of Israel throughout its history.

(a) The hope for a better future

Throughout Scripture, the "reign of God" is not another place, but another order—an order for which we hope, and which we can already touch and taste. No matter how surprising this might seem, Christian hope consists not in "going to heaven," but rather in having God's will be done "on earth as it is in heaven." Nor is the reign limited to certain things—those that are spiritual—leaving others (the material) aside. Just as the reign does not consist in "another place," nor is it limited to "other things." The reign of God encompasses all—heaven and earth, bodies and spirits.

The notion that heaven is "another place," and that our hope consists in going to that other place, arises out of the common tendency to confuse the message of the Bible with Platonic and Gnostic religiosity that has plagued Christianity repeatedly. Plato had affirmed that, above this world where all is passing and where the senses deceive us, there is another world of "pure ideas," that is to say, of ultimate realities that do not change or pass away. When the early Christians went throughout the Greco-Roman world preaching about eternal life, that Platonic doctrine became a strong apologetic argument in order to defend the Christian hope for life eternal and a reign of God. Unfortunately, one of the consequences of the use of this argument was that many Christians began thinking of the reign of God as something "up there," in the "beyond," and not as a future promise.

Although later, when we deal with the scope of the Kingdom, we shall come back to this point, it is important to stress here that just as the reign of God is not characterized by being "beyond," neither is it characterized by being purely spiritual. In much of the earliest Christian literature—the writings of Irenaeus in the second century—as well as in the New Testament, Christian hope has an earthly dimension, for there is frequent reference to material abundance and physical contentment. It was only later that this earthly dimension was abandoned, and it became common to speak of a purely spiritual hope.

The vision of the reign as another place, and as purely spiritual, that is, as ontologically different from "this age," has appeared repeatedly in the history of the church. This is due above all to the Platonic and Gnostic influences that have been repeatedly mentioned. On the basis of these positions, sometimes the church has ignored material, political, and economic issues, claiming that they are not important. At other points it has sought to control government and society on the basis that, after all, the spiritual order should be above the material. Ultimately, such understandings of the reign contradict the very doctrine of God, for they seem to indicate that, quite apart from God, there is another creative power, and that there are things that are neither God's creation nor God's concern.

The practical importance of all this is that, if we tend to think of the reign of God as "another place," rather than as "another time" or "another order," or if we deem it to be purely spiritual, we shall have no reason to be concerned about this place, this world, this society, this life. Certainly, such an attitude contradicts much of the biblical message. Our hope is for a better future—for a future in which the will of God will be fully manifest and obeyed.

That hope, and the joy it produces, may be compared to the situation of a girl who sees her presents under a Christmas tree. The day when she will be able to open them is not here yet, and sometimes—because she is so young—she even has difficulty understanding how long she must wait. She knows that the presents are hers, and every time she can she goes and touches them, or she picks them up and shakes them, not only to try to find out what is in them, but also in order to enjoy some of the promised joy. In those days before Christmas, she rejoices in what is already hers, and in what is still not quite hers yet. She certainly knows that Christmas Day will arrive, and even though sometimes she wishes that it would be sooner, all that she can do now is rejoice in the hope for what is to come.

In the Gospels, Jesus says on the one hand that the reign of God is "among you" (Luke 17:21), and on the other hand that it is near, that it is at hand, but is not yet here (Matt. 4:17). The reign is a promise and a reality, just as the girl's presents before Christmas.

Both in the Old and in the New Testaments that hope for the reign of God and its fullness, even though always future, has a concrete present in which it is made manifest. In the Old Testament, the presence of God among humans was made concrete in the ark of the covenant, in the temple, in the life of the people when it is faithful to God. Later, the rabbis began speaking of the *shekinah* of God—God's glorious presence, God's dwelling among the people—as the present manifestation and future promise of God's presence. In the New Testament, that presence is in Jesus Christ and then in the Holy Spirit, so that the church can now enjoy some of the presence of God while awaiting the final consummation. In that consummation the *shekinah* or presence of God will be absolute, manifest, and direct. That is why toward the very end of the book of Revelation the promise is expressed in terms of that presence: "See, the home of God is among mortals. He will dwell with them; they will be his peoples, and God himself will be with them" (Rev. 21:3).

(b) The scope of the reign

Although some did understand the "day of the Lord" as the time when God would vindicate Israel among all the nations—especially those who oppressed Israel—throughout the Old Testament there is the hope for a new order that goes far beyond such vindication. The prophet Isaiah speaks of a time when even the most profound enmities of nature will be resolved: "The wolf shall live with the lamb, the leopard shall lie down with the kid, the calf and the lion and the fatling together, and a little child shall lead them" (Isa. 11:6).

Likewise, Paul speaks, not only of the salvation of believers, but of an entire creation that awaits its liberation: "The creation itself will be set free from its bondage to decay and will obtain the freedom of the glory of the children of God. We know that the whole creation has been groaning in labor pains until now; and not only the creation, but we ourselves, who have the first fruits of the Spirit" (Rom. 8:21-23).

This means that the reign of God, that future which God has promised, is much more than the salvation of souls, and encompasses much more than human souls. This is a point at which Christian eschatology must critique a significant aspect, if not of the actual proclamation of the church at large, at least of the most commonly held vision of the future for which we hope. For many believers, what we should expect is a reign of pure disincarnate souls, floating in the clouds, without any reference to the rest of creation. But that is not the case; Christian hope is hope in the liberation of an entire creation, which in some mysterious manner has been subject to corruption and also awaits its liberation. The reign of God will be a universal reign, encompassing all of creation, and in which not only believers, but every creature, in heaven as well as on earth, will do God's will. That is why we pray daily, as Jesus taught us: "Thy will be done on earth as it is in heaven."

(c) *The nature of the reign*

This leads us to consider, not only the scope, but also the nature of the reign. As we have already stated, the hope for the reign is not to be understood so much in terms of a "beyond" as in terms of a "then." It is not a different place, but rather a different order. It is not a matter of going to heaven and leaving earth behind, but of a new heaven and a new earth (Rev. 21:1). Significantly, when the Bible speaks about this hope, it employs mainly two metaphors: "reign" and "city." Both a reign and a city are political terms.

Actually, the very word *politics* comes from the Greek root *polis*, which means "city." When today we read in Revelation that John saw a new city, we think only of a place where many people dwell together. Any center of population is a city for us. But that was not the full meaning of the word in the first century. The *polis*, the city, was a political entity, a state. For the ancients, one of the most important inventions of humankind was precisely the *polis*, the city, society organized as a system of government and of relationships. That is why Aristotle claimed that a human being is "a political animal."

The Romans had the same sense of "city." For them, the city *par excellence* was Rome. The term *civilization* comes from a Latin root meaning "city," and therefore to "civilize" is the same as to "citify." That was the core of Rome's imperial ideology, for it felt that it was called to build cities, to civilize the entire Mediterranean basin. In creating their vast empire, the Romans were convinced that they were taking to the rest of humankind the benefits of their city, that is, of their political, economic, and social order.

Therefore, when John in Revelation refers to a "holy city" he is speaking, not only of a place where people live, but also of a political, social, and economic order under God's rule. Furthermore, much of the book of Revelation could be read as the conflict between two societies or two political orders: the actual order of Rome—the great harlot seated on the seven hills—and the order of the new Jerusalem, where God will rule. Therefore, it is not surprising that Roman authorities soon began persecuting Christianity, which they correctly considered subversive.

This implies that Christian hope looks to a new order, different from the present one. The present order—or, as the New Testament frequently calls it, "this age" (Matt. 13:22, 40; Mark 4:19; 16:8; Rom. 12:2; 1 Cor. 1:20; 2:6, 8; 2 Cor. 4:4; Gal. 1:4; Eph. 1:21; 6:12)—is characterized by the abuse of power, by greed, and by self-interest. In contrast, the order of the reign is one of love toward the outcast, the oppressed, the powerless, and every other person in need. Jesus himself describes this contrast as follows: "You know that among the Gentiles those whom they recognize as their rulers lord it over them, and their great ones are tyrants over them. But it is not so among you; but whoever wishes to become great among you must be your servant, and whoever wishes to be first among you must be slave of all. For the Son of Man came not to be served but to serve" (Mark 10:42-45).

Therefore, the first characteristic of this reign that is the essence of Christian hope is service to others, whereas what characterizes the reigns of "this age" is self-interest. Much of contemporary political theory is based on self-interest, arguing—probably correctly—that what binds a society together is a social contract that results (or claims that it results) in benefit to its participants.

The service of the reign, however, takes place within an order of justice. In "this age," service is very often an excuse for exploitation, for the powerful expect the powerless to serve them, but not vice versa. In the order of the reign, in contrast, there is no exploitation, but justice and equity.

The hope for justice is a central theme throughout the Bible. The psalmist sings of the promise that "faithfulness will spring up from the ground, and righteousness [or justice] will look down from the sky . . . righteousness [or justice] will go before him" (Ps. 85:11-13). The prophet Isaiah, upon rejoicing that "a child has been born for us, a son given to us; authority rests upon his shoulders," also declares that this child will sit upon the throne of David, and that "he will establish and uphold it with justice and with righteousness from this time onward and forevermore" (Isa. 9:6-7). And later, referring to the "cornerstone," which God has laid in Zion, he adds: "And I will make justice the line, and righteousness the plummet" (Isa. 28:17; see also Isa. 32:16; 42:1, 6-7; 51:5-6; and others). Likewise, the theme of justice as promised by God appears throughout the prophets (see Jer. 23:5; 33:15). In the New Testament, Jesus tells his disciples: "Blessed are those who hunger and thirst for righteousness [or justice], for they will be filled" (Matt. 5:6), and on speaking of the task of the disciples, he tells them that above all they are to seek "the kingdom of God and his righteousness" (Matt. 6:33).

Furthermore, this justice does not consist only, or even mainly, in punishing the evil and rewarding the good, but is rather the establishment of a new order in which all shall benefit from the bounty of creation. That is why prophet Micah, in describing "the last days," affirms that "they shall all sit under their own vines and under their own fig trees" (Mic. 4:4). In similar fashion, another prophet affirms that "on that day, says the LORD of hosts, you shall invite each other to come under your vine and fig tree" (Zech. 3:10).

Besides such just distribution of goods, the reign of God is also characterized by peace. In "this age," efforts to establish justice are too frequently accompanied by violence and destruction. But what Christian hope promises is a reign of justice with peace. The vision of the "peaceable kingdom" of Isaiah 11 has already been quoted, in which "the wolf shall live with the lamb." Elsewhere (32:17) Isaiah says that "the effect of righteousness will be peace, and the result of righteousness, quietness and trust forever." And the psalmist sings about the day when "righteousness and peace will kiss each other" (Ps. 85:10).

Part of this peace is consolation, and the end to suffering. Paul says that all of creation as well as "we ourselves" are in pain as of childbirth, awaiting the day of our liberation from such pain. Revelation promises that "he will wipe every tear from their eyes. Death will be no more; mourning and crying and pain will be no more, for the first things have passed away" (Rev. 21:4).

In summary, the reign consists in a new order under God's rule, and is characterized by service, justice, peace, consolation, and joy. Everything that opposes this—exploitation, injustice, violence, pain, and sadness—is part of "this age," which shall pass. All of this is summarized by speaking of the direct presence of God, for all of these characteristics of the reign are also typical of God's action throughout history. That is why the seer at Patmos declares that in the holy city there is no temple, for "its temple is the Lord God the Almighty and the Lamb" (Rev. 21:22).

(d) Citizens of God's reign

Although the reign is a promise of God for the future, in a certain sense it is already a reality. It is a reality, because it has been inaugurated with the resurrection of Jesus Christ and the gift of the Holy Spirit. And it is also a reality because those who believe in the promise must now live as citizens of the reign of God (Phil. 3:20; Heb. 11:13-16). Christian hope produces in us, not only trust and firmness in the faith, but also a different way of living. Giving "an account of the hope" that is in us (1 Pet. 3:15) is not only a matter of being able to explain it, but also and above all living out of that hope.

Unfortunately, too often eschatological hope has been used as an excuse to avoid the difficult decisions of life, and especially not to face the injustices of the present order. Such has been the case when it has been thought that God's reign is a "beyond" where the souls of the saved dwell, and that it has nothing to do with the rest of creation, or with the social and economic order. We are then told that, if there is now hunger or oppression, we are not to be too concerned, for in heaven there shall be abundance and freedom. ("Pie in the sky, by and by.") And we are also told that, since it is only the soul that will be saved, whatever happens to bodies is only of secondary importance. On the basis of what has been said above about the scope of the reign, it is clear that this is an error, for the reign includes the entirety of creation, and rather than a beyond, is a different order.

In a way, life is always lived from a hope or an expectation. We make decisions today on the basis of where we expect or hope to be tomorrow. Whoever really expects something, in a way already lives it. Whoever expects to travel prepares luggage and studies the places to be visited. If someone tells us that he or she is planning a trip, but makes no reservations, buys no tickets, and does not pack, we doubt that such plans really exist. Likewise, whoever expects the reign of God will live now, in the present age, out of that hope, and will give indications that such is the case.

Thus, if one of the characteristics of the reign is love, Christian life must be loving. If another characteristic is peace, every fight and enmity are opposed to it, and whoever lives out of the hope of the reign will seek peace and reconciliation. If it is characterized by justice, whoever claims to be a citizen of the reign will struggle against every injustice in "this age." If it is characterized by the presence of God, Christian life will be, not only in the future, but already now, a life in the constant presence of God.

Paul declares that "we wait for adoption, the redemption of our bodies" (Rom. 8:23). God has adopted us as children, and what we await is the culmination of that adoption in the reign, when we shall come into our inheritance. Meanwhile, we are to live as children of God.

There is a popular saying, "like father, like son" (which could also be "like mother, like daughter"). What we mean by that is that children reflect the character, the talents, attitudes, and values of their parents. In a way, whoever has not met our parents gets to know something about them through us. Likewise, those who do not know God attain a glimpse of the divine nature and will through those who claim to be children of God—just as we have known God by means of the only begotten Son, Jesus. Therefore, when we claim to be children of God, citizens of the reign, we take upon ourselves the burden of behaving as such, for we thereby announce the reign, prepare to live in it, and give witness of the character and the purposes of our heavenly Parent.

Note, however, that we do not claim that our task is to bring the reign of God, or even to build it. The reign of God is not a human work or construction, but is God's. Too frequently Christians have imagined that they can bring God's reign on earth. In most cases, this has resulted in policies of oppression and persecution that hardly witness to the love of God. At any rate, it is a usurpation of the power and authority of God. The reign is "of God," not only in the sense that it is God's rule, but also in the sense that it is God's doing.

4. ETERNAL LIFE

Up to this point we have hardly mentioned what for many people is the very heart of eschatology, that is, eternal life. Life after death, heaven, and hell, have captivated the imagination of people throughout the ages. Painters, poets, and preachers have depicted overwhelming pictures of life in heaven or in hell, so that in any museum and in many churches we find paintings in which beautiful angels float around the clouds, sometimes in the company of the saints, praising God with harps and trumpets. And we also see bloodcurdling paintings in which demonic and deformed beings torture the souls of the condemned in hell. Although today such paintings are studied as part of the history of art, those who produced them did not have purely aesthetic purposes. They actually wished to remind us that death hovers over each of us, and that we must give some consideration to what comes after it. Therefore, while people were invited to imagine the torments of hell or the pleasures of heaven, they were invited to live the present life with a view to the future one.

Although such visions of life after death may not have today the impact that they did in the past, and even though much of what they taught us may be doubted, they at least serve to affirm a central point in Christian doctrine: death does not have the final word. This is not because the soul is immortal, but rather because God is a God of life, whose will is not for death, but for life.

Although most people do not realize it, the immortality of the soul is not a Christian doctrine, nor does it appear in the Bible. On the contrary, the Bible certainly considers the soul to be mortal (Ezek. 18:4, 20; Matt. 10:28; James 5:20). In the Bible, immortality is not a characteristic that belongs to the soul itself, but is rather a gift of God. Furthermore, when it refers to the future life, Christian hope speaks not only of the life of the soul, but also of the resurrection of the body. What has happened in this case, as in so many others, is that when Christianity began its preaching in the Greco-Roman world there were already theories of the immortality of the soul—an immortality that had been held, among others, by Socrates and by Plato. Therefore, in order to show that life after death was not as irrational as some claimed, some Christians began relating it with the Platonic theory of the immortality of the soul. Eventually, that relationship was such that many came to think that what the Bible speaks about when referring to eternal life is the same as the immortality of the soul as it was taught by the great philosophers of antiquity.

In the Bible, God's intention is life. That is why in the Garden of Eden there is, besides the tree of knowledge of good and evil, the tree of life. It is after sin that God closes to humanity the path to the tree of life (Gen. 3:22-24). But even so, the tree that is forbidden in Genesis is promised in Revelation, where it appears in the middle of the new Jerusalem, and where its leaves are for the healing of nations (Rev. 22:2). And, since God's intention is not for death, but for life, the Bible also affirms "the hope of eternal life that God, who never lies, promised before the ages began" (Titus 1:2).

Certainly, part of Christian hope—of that hope that is not a mere yearning, but a security grounded on God's promises—is the continuation of life into eternity, even beyond death.

The promise and reality of eternal life are not limited to the continuation of life for an indefinite time, but rather include also a way of living that the Bible calls "life abundant" (John 10:10). Such a life does not begin with death, but rather with our new birth in Christ, and it comes to fruition at the time of our presence with him in glory. The First Epistle of John declares that "God gave us eternal life, and this life is in his Son. Whoever has the Son has life; whoever does not have the Son of God does not have life" (1 John 5:11-12). Paul expresses it in other words, affirming that whoever is a Christian is already dead to the old life: "You have died, and your life is hidden with Christ in God. When Christ who is your life is revealed, then you also will be revealed with him in glory" (Col. 3:3-4). It is then a matter of a quality of life grounded on the knowledge and the experience of God's love and fidelity—which are definitively manifested in the incarnation, death, and resurrection of Jesus Christ. This life consists in loving and being loved by the one who is the only perfect love. In other words, the eternal life that we already enjoy is a foretaste of the life in the reign, and must therefore be a life of love, peace, service, and justice. To live "in Christ" is to live as one who knows that one's true life is hidden with Christ, awaiting the glorious manifestation of Christ and of God's reign.

Part of this life consists in victory over death. This is not because the soul is immortal by nature—which it is not—but rather because God is a God of life. This has been clearly manifested in the victory of Jesus Christ over death, which is the first fruits of our own resurrection, and therefore we can say with Paul: "Where, O death, is your victory? Where, O death, is your sting? . . . But thanks be to God, who gives us the victory through our Lord Jesus Christ" (1 Cor. 15:56-57).

As was said above, the Christian hope of life after death is expressed, not in terms of the immortality of the soul, but rather in terms of the resurrection of the body. This is what the Apostles' Creed affirms, where we declare that we believe "in the resurrection of the body and life everlasting." "Life everlasting" is life that culminates after "the resurrection of the body."

The difference between the theory of the immortality of the soul and the Christian doctrine of the resurrection of the body is important at least for two reasons. The first of these is that we do affirm that our hope of life is not based on ourselves, or on our own supposedly immortal nature, but is rather based on the resurrection of Jesus Christ. It is by his victory over death that those who join him as members of his body know that we shall live with him. The second is that we do affirm that the purposes of God include, not only souls and "spiritual" realities, but all of our existence. God loves us and promises us that we shall live, not merely as disincarnate souls, but as full human beings.

Such eternal life does not come to us through our merits, nor is it an award for an earthly life of good deeds, but is rather a free gift of God. The God of life invites us to have communion with God, and thus to partake of the abundant life that only God can give.

We also know that God does not force human will. Even though God is a God of life, there is always the possibility of choosing the anti-God, death. Although God is a God of justice, it is always possible to insist on injustice, and to rejoice in it. Although God offers and promises life, it is always possible to reject those promises.

God is not only a God of love, but also a God of justice. One of the great dilemmas throughout the history of Christian theology has been how to coordinate these two facets or aspects of God's nature. From the human point of view, there seems to be a contradiction, or at least a very strong tension, between these two. If God is love, and this love is manifested in grace and forgiveness, the logical consequence is that all will be saved, and that in the end all will enjoy the life that God gives. If God is just, the logical consequence is that God will punish those who reject the offer of a new life.

The Bible expresses God's justice in terms of the final judgment and eternal condemnation. The theme of judgment appears repeatedly in the Bible, and we cannot ignore it simply because we find it difficult to join it to our experience of God's love. In Revelation, John says: "And I saw the dead, great and small, standing before the throne. . . . And the dead were judged according to their works, as recorded in the books. . . . And anyone whose name was not found written in the book of life was thrown into the lake of fire" (Rev. 20:12-15). Jesus himself speaks of the judgment of the nations, when all the nations will stand before him. Part of the final verdict of that judgment is, "Depart from me into the eternal fire prepared for the devil and his angels" (Matt. 25:41). And elsewhere in the New Testament there is reference to "weeping and gnashing of teeth" (Matt. 8:12; 13:42, 50; 22:13; 24:58; 25:30; Luke 13:28). These and many other texts claim or imply that those who do not accept God's mercy and forgiveness will be condemned for eternity.

This "eternal fire," "lake of fire," or place of "weeping and gnashing of teeth" has traditionally been associated with the notion of hell. The words *inferno* and *infernal* come from the same root as *inferior,* and simply refer to hell as "the lower parts" of creation. This comes from the vision of antiquity, of a world in three stories. The earth on which we live was the intermediate level, with heaven above and the inferior places, or hell, below. This is the worldview to which Paul refers in declaring that before the name of Jesus every knee will bend "in heaven and on earth and under the earth" (Phil. 2:10), that is to say, everywhere.

The traditional notion of hell does not appear in the Old Testament, but is partly a development of the Hebrew notion of *Sheol.* The Sheol or "abyss" in most of the Old Testament is the place where the dead reside, and even though it is a place of darkness, it is usually not described as a place of torment or of fire—except later, in the apocryphal books of the Old Testament. In the New Testament, the words that are most commonly employed to refer to hell are *Gehenna* and *Hades.* The first derives from the valley of Hinom, where in ancient times Gentiles sacrificed children through fire in honor of Moloch. The second refers to the place of the dead, like the Hebrew Sheol. It is interesting to note that in Revelation 20:14 John declares that "death and Hades were thrown into the lake of fire." Throughout history, Christians have debated the place of hell in Christian hope. Whereas most have simply accepted the biblical witness regarding eternal punishment, others have insisted that God's power and love are such that in the end all will be saved. This position is usually called "universalism"—that is, the notion that salvation is universal. Although several ancient theologians held such a position, the best known among them was Origen. According to Origen, the fire of damnation is not eternal, but is rather like a purifying fire, whose purpose is to make the sinner worthy of being in the presence of God. At the end all will be saved—and this includes not only human sinners, but even the demons, for otherwise the power of God would be frustrated. The Almighty God of Scripture is to triumph over every sort of evil.

Although universalism was rejected by the ancient church, it has repeatedly resurfaced, and in modern times has gained many followers. Furthermore, although the Bible without doubt speaks of an eternal damnation, there are also certain passages that seem to promise a universal redemption. Paul says that "just as one man's trespass led to condemnation for all, so one man's act of righteousness leads to justification and life for all" (Rom. 5:18). And he also says that "as all die in Adam, so all will be made alive in Christ" (1 Cor. 15:22).

In the last analysis, the question regarding the existence of hell refers to the nature of God. Hell, no matter how one understands it, must not be thought of as a place completely alien to God's power. That is why the psalmist declares, "If I make my bed in Sheol, you are there" (Ps. 139:8). And Jesus declares about his church that "the gates of Hades will not prevail against it" (Matt. 16:18).

Regarding the existence and permanence of hell, three positions are possible. Some insist on the almighty love of God, which they feel is contradicted by an eternal damnation, for this would leave some creatures beyond the reach of God's redemptive power. Those who affirm the existence of an eternal damnation declare, not only that the Bible speaks about such damnation repeatedly, but also that God is just, and that God's justice cannot be evaded. While the salvation of some shows God's love, the damnation of others shows God's justice. As a third alternative, it is possible to say simply that, although there is no doubt that God is love, and even though from our human perspective eternal damnation does not seem to be compatible with such love, in God love and justice agree in a mysterious way that our mind is not able to fathom. The value of this third position is that it helps us center our attention where it should be. Too often, the question of eternal salvation and damnation becomes the center of the preaching of the gospel. In such cases, the point is even reached where the "good news" begins with the claim that "if you don't believe, you will burn in hell." Certainly, the good news is the gift of eternal life through Jesus our Lord, but it goes far beyond our own salvation. The good news is the hope of redemption, not only for us, but also for the entire creation (Rom. 8:21). The good news is that the God of life has conquered death through the crucifixion and resurrection of Jesus Christ. This good news calls us to love the God of life, not just because God promises life eternal, but simply because God is love. As was dramatically stated by an anonymous Spanish poet in the sixteenth century:

My God, I love Thee, not because
I hope for heav'n thereby,
nor yet because who love Thee not
must die eternally.

Thou, O my Jesus, Thou didst me
upon the cross embrace.
For me didst bear the nails and spear,
and manifold disgrace.

Then why, O blessed Jesus Christ,
should I not love Thee well?
Not for the hope of winning heav'n
or of escaping hell;

Not with the hope of gaining aught;
not seeking a reward;
but as Thyself hast loved me,
O ever-loving Lord! [1]

1. Translated from an anonymous sonnet, *"No me mueve, mi Dios, para quererte."* Full text in *The Hymnal* (Philadelphia: Presbyterian Board of Education, 1935), #313. Translated from Latin in 1849 by Edward Caswall, but the sonnet originated in Spain in the sixteenth century.

AUTHORS CITED

Abelard, Peter (1079–1142). One of the main promoters of the intellectual renaissance of the twelfth century, and a forerunner of Scholasticism. He was known for his sharp use of logic, which earned him the enmity of many.

Anselm of Canterbury (Saint Anselm, 1033–1109). A philosopher and theologian of the eleventh century, considered one of the fathers of Scholastic theology, which held sway in the schools and universities for the rest of the Middle Ages. Known for his "ontological" proof of the existence of God and for his clear statement of the substitutionary theory of atonement.

Apollinaris (ca. 310—ca. 390). Bishop of Laodicea in Syria. An exponent of the type of Christology that is usually associated with Alexandria. His teachings on this subject were rejected by the Council of Constantinople (381 C.E.).

Arius (ca. 250–336). A presbyter from Alexandria whose doctrines gave rise to the Arian controversy. He held that the Word is not eternal and is not God, but was created by God as the first of all creatures. The Council of Nicea (325) rejected his doctrines. It was mostly against them that the Nicene Creed was composed.

Augustine (Saint Augustine, 354–430). A native of North Africa, and bishop of Hippo in that region after 395. Possibly the most influential theologian in the entire history of the Western church. He is particularly remarkable for his doctrine of grace, through which he influenced the Protestant reformers of the sixteenth century. Two of his main works are *Confessions* and *City of God*.

Aulén, Gustaf (1879–1977). A Swedish Lutheran theologian who, together with other Swedish Lutherans, established at the University of Lund what came to be known as the Lundensian school of theology.

Averroës (1126–1198). A Muslim philosopher and jurist. He was particularly known as an interpreter and commentator on the philosophy of Aristotle. His works had a great impact on Christian Europe in the thirteenth century.

Barth, Karl (1886–1968). A pastor and theologian, probably the most important Protestant theologian of the twentieth century. His *Commentary on Romans* changed the course of theology, overcoming the liberal theology that had held sway until then. His theological school is usually called "neo-orthodox," "dialectical theology," and "theology of crisis." He was staunchly opposed to Nazism. He underscored divine transcendence and sovereignty above every human effort, be it in theology or in politics. His main work is *Church Dogmatics*.

Basil of Caesarea (Saint Basil, ca. 330–379). Bishop of that city, also known as "Basil the Great." A theologian who was particularly known for his defense of trinitarian doctrine, and especially for his work *On the Holy Spirit*. One of the main organizers of Eastern monasticism.

Bonaventura (Saint Bonaventura, ca.1217–1274). A leading theologian and Franciscan mystic, general and reorganizer of the Franciscan order. He rejected the extreme Aristotelianism of the Averroists, emphasizing faith and contemplation above reason, and insisting on the Augustinian tradition over against the new Aristotelian tendencies of his time.

Bultmann, Rudolf (1884–1976). A German scholar of the New Testament. He was very much influenced by the philosophy of Heidegger. His main proposal was the "demythologization" of the New Testament, in order to make its message more accessible to modern people.

Calixtus (?–ca. 223). Bishop of Rome from approximately 217 to the time of his death. Hippolytus accused him of being too lax in forgiving and readmitting to Communion those who had committed fornication.

Calvin, John (1509–1564). A French reformer and theologian who helped organize and direct the Reformation in Geneva. He was the great theologian and systematizer of Protestant teaching, and particularly of the Reformed tradition, which considers him its main theologian. His most important work is *Institutes of the Christian Religion*.

Clement of Alexandria (ca. 150–ca. 215). A theologian from that city who used the Platonic philosophical tradition for his defense and his interpretation of Christian faith. He was known for his allegorical interpretation of Scripture.

Copernicus, Nicolaus (1473–1543). An astronomer who proposed the theory of a solar system revolving around the sun, by which he contradicted the accepted views of his time.

Cyprian (?–258). Bishop of Carthage in North Africa. He is particularly known for his treatises on the nature of the church and for his controversies with the bishop of Rome over the rebaptism of Novatian schismatics (see below: Novatian).

Darwin, Charles (1809–1882). Proponent of the theory of evolution regarding the origin of species. Although originally a religious man and a promoter of Christian missions, as time went by he became increasingly agnostic.

Francis of Assisi (Saint Francis, 1181–1226). Founder of the order of Franciscans. He insisted on voluntary poverty, simplicity, and love for all.

Galileo (1564–1642). An Italian astronomer and mathematician. His support of the Copernican theory of the solar system led to his eventual imprisonment by the Inquisition.

Gregory of Nazianzus (329–389). One of the "great Cappadocians" (jointly with Basil of Caesarea and Gregory of Nyssa). Together with them, he defended the Nicene faith against Arianism.

Gregory of Nyssa (ca. 329–395). Bishop of that small city, in what today is Turkey. A defender of trinitarian doctrine in the controversies that eventually led to the Council of Constantinople (381). He is known above all as a mystical theologian.

Hegel, G. W. F. (1770–1831). A German philosopher of the Idealist tradition. According to him, history is the unfolding of the universal mind, so that history reveals that mind. His impact on theology was significant, for it seemed to many that he had finally organized the totality of reality and of existence into a single system. (It was against that system that Kierkegaard wrote some of his best works.)

Hermas (second century). A Christian author who lived in Rome in the middle of the second century, and a brother to the bishop of that city. His work, *The Shepherd*, in which he tells his visions, is the most extensive among the "Apostolic Fathers."

Hippolytus (ca. 170–235). An outstanding scholar, theologian, martyr, and leader of the Roman Church, and the first "anti-pope" recorded. His *Apostolic Tradition* gives important details about worship in the Roman Church in his time. He clashed with Calixtus on the issue of the restoration of the lapsed.

Ignatius of Antioch (ca. 35–107). Bishop of Antioch in Syria who died a martyr in Rome during the reign of Trajan (98–117). He wrote seven letters while on his way to martyrdom, and these offer us a significant window into the life and devotion of the time.

Irenaeus (second century). Bishop of Lyons. A staunch opponent of Gnosticism. His two major works are one of our best sources for the earliest Christian theology.

John Scotus Erigena (ca. 810–880). The most distinguished philosopher of the ninth century. He tried to organize all of reality within a single system on the basis of the Platonic and mystical traditions. He was accused of pantheism.

Justin Martyr (ca. 100–165). After searching for the "true philosophy" among pagan philosophers, he was converted to Christianity. He was the most important of Christian apologists during the second century, and tried to show the compatibility of Christian faith with pagan philosophy, on the basis of the doctrine of the Logos. He died a martyr in Rome.

Kierkegaard, Søren (1813–1855). A Danish writer and theologian whose works gave rise to existentialism. A man of profound religiosity, he wrote especially against the rationalism of the Hegelian "System" and against the manner in which the Danish Church had accommodated itself to the expectations of society.

Luther, Martin (1483–1546). German reformer. Formerly an Augustinian monk, he came to the conviction that salvation is by faith, by the grace of God, and not by works or by merits. For that reason he protested against the sale of indulgences. He spent most of his life as a professor at the University of Wittenberg.

Marcion (second century). He proposed the theory of an absolute contrast between the God of the Old Testament and the God of the New—one is just and punishing, and the other loving and forgiving. According to him, only Paul really understood the gospel of grace. His New Testament consisted of the Gospel of Luke and the Letters of Paul—although eliminating all quotes and references to the Old Testament.

Melanchthon, Philipp (1497–1560). A companion and follower of Luther, whose work he continued after the death of the reformer. More moderate than Luther, sometimes his own moderation led to controversies with the stricter Lutherans.

Nestorius (?–ca. 452). Patriarch of Constantinople, and exponent of Antiochene Christology, who distinguished between the two natures of Christ in such a way that he seemed to divide the Savior into two persons. The Council of Ephesus (431) rejected his doctrines and deposed him.

Novatian (middle of the third century). A Roman presbyter who in the year 251 abandoned the rest of the church in that city and gave origin to the rigorous movement of the Novatians. His followers continued existing separately at least until the fifth century.

Origen (ca. 185–254). A prolific author of Platonic inspiration, and a follower of Clement of Alexandria. A native of that city, he spent most of his life there, until he moved to Caesarea in his latter years. Like Clement, he interpreted the Bible allegorically. One of his main works is the *Hexapla*, a Bible with six parallel columns comparing various versions. His theories regarding the Godhead set the stage for the Arian controversy, more than fifty years after his death.

Plato (427–347 B.C.E). A Greek philosopher, a disciple and interpreter of Socrates. He established the famous "Academy" of Athens, where he taught philosophy, and which continued existing until the year 529 C.E. His theories regarding "ideas" or "forms" that are universal, and of which particular things participate, were very influential in the course of Christian theology.

Ritschl, Albrecht (1822–1889). A German Protestant theologian, and a leader of liberal theology. He stressed moral life as the very center of religion. The purpose of God's revelation in Jesus Christ is to call us to that moral life.

Spener, Philipp Jacob (1635–1705). The founder of German Pietism. In his main work, *Pia Desideria*, he proposed organizing small "colleges of piety," which would be groups devoted to supporting one another in cultivating Christian piety. Pietism was influential in giving new zeal to the missionary movement.

Tertullian (ca. 160–225). Probably a native of Carthage, in North Africa, where he spent most of his life and where he apparently was a lawyer. He was converted as an adult. He is considered the "father of Latin theology," for he developed much of the Latin theological vocabulary. He wrote defending Christianity in the face of persecutions, and also against Gnosticism and the doctrines of Marcion.

Thomas à Kempis (ca. 1380–1471). An ascetic and mystical writer who was very influential in the last years of the Middle Ages through his famous book *Imitation of Christ*.

Thomas Aquinas (1225–1274). A Dominican philosopher and theologian. He responded positively to the introduction of Aristotelianism in Western theology, creating a synthesis between that philosophical system and Christian faith—a synthesis now called "Thomism." Although at first his doctrines were rejected, eventually his theology became the most influential in the Roman Catholic Church. His principal writing is *Summa Theologica*. He was declared a "doctor of the church" in 1563.

Vincent of Lérins (?–ca. 449). A monk who resisted the "innovations" of Saint Augustine, insisting on the authority of tradition and on the importance of human effort in salvation.

Wesley, John (1703–1791). The founder of the Methodist movement within the Church of England, and through it eventually of the various Methodist, Wesleyan, and Holiness churches. He stressed the importance of commitment to the gospel, a personal experience with Christ, the process of sanctification, and the social impact of Christian faith.

Zanchi, Jerome (1516–1590). An Italian Protestant theologian who taught at Strasbourg and Heidelberg. He was a staunch defender of the most rigid predestination, as may be seen in his work *The Doctrine of Absolute Predestination*.

Zwingli, Ulrich (1484–1531). A Swiss reformer, organizer, and leader of the Reformation in Zurich. The earliest theologian of what eventually became the Reformed tradition. He was strongly influenced by humanism and by its emphasis on returning to the sources, and therefore he rejected everything that was not to be found in the Bible. His interpretation of the presence of Christ in the Eucharist as symbolic rather than real led to a strong disagreement with Luther.